Choices

the crossroads between

yesterday,

today

and

tomorrow

Tecia Farmer Janes

Cover Illustration: K Harman Designs, LLC
Amanda Snow

ISBN 10: 1499361629
ISBN 13: 9781499361629

Contents

CONTENTS

Acknowledgments

To *Russ*, my wonderful husband, it was your unwavering encouragement and support that pushed me to complete this study in the midst of working and going to school. I could not and would not have done this without you. I love you.

To my kids, *Matthew* and *Olivia*, thank you for supporting me and pitching in to give me time to write. You both have taught me so much and continue to teach me as each day passes. You are my greatest blessing and greatest joy. I love you both.

To my sister, *Kasey Hanson*, who held me accountable to stay with it, encouraged me and refocused me when the going got tough. I love you and I am so grateful for you in my life.

To my mom, *Tyra Walker*, thank you for being the example of Christ in my life. I love you.

To my sister, *Keri Davis*, for being a perfect example of perseverance and running the race set before us. Thank you *Keri,* for your willingness to be my final editor. I love you.

To my mother-in-love, Brenda Janes, thank you for being my biggest cheerleader. Your encouragement, love and support are a true treasure in my life.

To my mentors and friends, *Ms. Pat McBurnett, Ms. Chris Elliott, Darlene Burnett, Julie Boyd, Kristie Washington, Christine Thompson and Laurie Kollar,* who helped edit, support, love and pray me through this project, I am forever grateful.

To the *Southcrest Women's Bible Study Groups* that piloted this study to help make it the best it can be, Thank you.

To my *Lord and Savior*, I am humbled beyond measure that You enabled and allowed me to write about You. You guided, disciplined, loved and allowed me to see more of You on this journey. To know more of You is my greatest reward.

About the Author

"...Teach me your ways so I may know You...."
Exodus 33:13

Tecia Farmer Janes is an inspiring author, speaker, teacher, wife and mother of two wonderful children. Tecia was introduced and accepted Christ at an early age. In her teen years, her faith was deepened and tested through the sudden and tragic loss of her father. During this time, Tecia began to cling to God and her love for His word sustained her during the hardest times of her life. Through daily choices of love, forgiveness, obedience, surrendering, sacrificing and trust, she began seeking a deeper relationship with Christ. Tecia received a degree in Christian Ministry from Point University, which helped to flame her desire to encourage women to study God's word for themselves. She is passionate about connecting our lives with the people of the Bible while teaching others how to pursue a personal and contagious faith.

Introduction

Choices are one thing we all have in common. We make choices every day in order to live. Choices are one of the greatest gifts God has given us. We have choices like do we want ice cream or brownies for dessert, who we get to marry, where we live and work, but especially the choice to accept the love and sacrifice that Jesus offers us. God loved us enough that He created us and then gave us the gift of choice. God desired a relationship with each of us. A relationship means that each chooses the other. Accepting Christ as Savior is one choice; it is another choice to live out our daily lives with Him. The choice to love Jesus is a gift. Choosing to live a life that grows daily into a deeper relationship with Christ is a level of living that He wants so desperately for us to begin. The choice to choose God with our every decision is sometimes made daily or at desperate times chosen one minute and one breath at a time. When we grow and deepen our relationship with God, we build our own history with Him. When we choose to love, obey, forgive, sacrifice, trust, and surrender control, we begin to see His faithfulness in every detail of our lives.

Life is full of events. There are many joys and many sorrows that you will experience throughout your life. Have you ever felt like you were on your very own roller coaster of life? There are ups and downs and curves that you aren't prepared for. There are times when you want to get off and times when you want to stay on and ride again. Riding alone can be quite scary. Fear is often amplified when we are alone, but so is the thrill when we are able to share it. The experience can be totally different depending on whom you're with. Your story is something you share with others when you return. If you choose to ride alone, then you could miss the connection with others as they share their experiences. You might have been on the same ride and the circumstances could be the same, but the feelings you experienced might be different from the others. You felt alone in your journey.

We often feel alone in life, but the reality is someone is in the seat in front of you, who took this ride just a little ahead of you. You can choose to share your journey with someone who can support you and guide you along the way.

This is what the Bible is all about. It's the story that was written about people just like you and me. They may have lived in an earlier time, but they experienced the same feelings, actions, and decisions as we do today. Satan tries to convince us that we are alone in this world and that no one knows what we are going through. Just like on the roller coaster, Satan blinds us to those who are in the seat in front of us. When we open our eyes in the sharp curves and look ahead, we realize there are people on this ride with us. God chose to give us a book full of other peoples' stories so their lives could guide us and encourage us to stay on course. He wants us to know we are not alone and that He is the reason so many people of yesterday made decisions freeing them, and the generations to come. The Bible is full of people who made some very hard choices to go with God on this roller coaster called life. Our choices become the crossroads between yesterday, today, and tomorrow.

How This Study Works

Choices is a six-week study including five days of homework each week. We will look at some of the difficult choices people in the Bible had to make and how those choices impacted those around them as well as generations to come. Each week presents a unique choice arising from struggles that are as real to us today as they were back then. We will dive into scripture and unearth God's truth in real-life examples. Each week holds its own treasure. The outline of the study uses the following consistent structure:

Each week the "Choice" will be introduced. There will be a weekly scripture that will highlight the concept of each choice. I encourage each one of you to memorize these verses. You can put these on a card and carry it in your car, or write it on your mirror. When we have verses memorized they are ready to encourage us at the perfect time.

Group Discussion Questions. These same questions will appear each week and will be discussed within your group the next time you meet. Keep these questions in your mind as you go through the week so that you can contribute to your group.

Days 1, 2, and 3, looks into the life of a person in the Bible who struggled when presented with a specific choice. Some made the good choice to go with God, others made the choice to do it alone. We will look at their circumstances and the details of their lives. We will discover what was involved in the choices they were being asked to make. The opportunity to know each person, who sat in the seat before us, offers us the advantage of seeing the end of their story while we live ours out. They had to live life day-to-day as they made their choices, without the advantage of an example before them. Their choices to love, obey, forgive, surrender, sacrifice, and trust provided the guardrails for their roller coaster during their lives.

Day 4. We will look at Jesus. Jesus never asks us to do anything that He Himself did not do while He was here on earth. Jesus felt just like we feel; He was tempted as we are tempted; and He hurt just like we hurt. On the fourth day of each week, we will look deep into Jesus's life and the specific choices Jesus faced.

Day 5. This is where the head knowledge of the week becomes the heart knowledge of today and tomorrow. We will look at areas where God is calling us to make hard choices. We will draw strength from those who have gone before us and use their examples to see how we should move forward today. This will require honesty and reflection on your part. If you skip this day, then you might miss the blessing of seeing God work in your life in these areas.

I am so excited to take this journey with you. I pray you will dig deep into God's Word and allow Him to be your source of strength. My heart's desire is for each of us to become so comfortable and so personal with God and His Word that we can't live a day without it. There are so many wonderful studies to assist us in understanding, but if we skip the Bible and rely only on the interpretation of others, then we can miss the amazing journey of seeing God in our details and in our story. Learn to dig deep into the Bible yourself—it was given to us as a lifeline. Let's embrace this blessing for ourselves! I am praying for each of you that you will experience God like you have never before. May we be forever changed as we choose to live lives that reflect the heart of God.

Choosing Him,
Tecia

CHOICES Leader's Guide

Thank you so much for taking this journey and for leading others down this path. When we realize that we have choices in our lives, our outlook on life changes from a victim mentality to that of a victor, all because of Christ. When we choose Him, everything else takes its rightful place behind Him.

Each week examines a different struggle that we all experience. The goal of this study is to help us see the crossroads of choices that were around in the past and are around us today. The devil's greatest lie is that we are alone in this world and that no one knows how we feel. The Bible is full of stories of people who felt like we do and had to make the same choices we face. The goal of this study is to tie the threads together, from the people of the Bible to us today. In doing this, we will be able to draw strength from their choices and their results. Each person made his or her choice one day at a time, just like we do. They did not get to see the end results of their choices as history allows us to see. Seeing their success and failures should be a huge resource and strength for us.

- Each week there is a verse to memorize. This verse is the foundation of the week's study. Encourage the participants to write these verses on a card and post them in your kitchen or car, use a dry erase marker to write it on your mirror or anywhere they will be seen frequently through the week.

- For six weeks we will study a different person for the first three days. The fourth day will always be a look at Jesus, and the fifth day will always be a personal application crucial to understanding our choices.

- Each week you will answer the same set of questions with regard to that week's topic found in the Group Discussion Questions, as well as the questions provided in the leaders guide.

Be prepared to answer these questions with your group next week.

- Which person in the Bible did you relate to the most this week?

- Is there another person in the Bible who made this same choice? Who?

- How do their circumstances relate to yours?

- What changes will you make in your life by choosing to love, forgive, obey, surrender, sacrifice and trust?

My prayer for each of us is that we begin to draw strength from the people of the Bible who made the choice to go with God. Take the participants into the lives of each biblical person, their family, and their feelings. Then look at the choices they made despite their feelings. Each week, help your participants to relate to the stories so that they can be encouraged and draw strength from each choice made.

Thank you for being willing vessels to walk alongside today's people of the Bible.

Choosing Him,
Tecia

The Choice to Love

Group Discussion Questions

Be prepared to answer these questions with your group next week.

1. Which person in the Bible did you relate to the most this week?

_____

_____

_____

_____

_____

_____

2. Is there another person in the Bible who made this same choice? Who?

_____

_____

_____

_____

_____

_____

3. How do their circumstances relate to yours?

_____

_____

_____

_____

_____

_____

4. What changes will you make in your life by choosing to love?

_____

_____

_____

_____

_____

_____

WEEK 1: LOVE

Leaders's Questions for Week One: The Choice to Love
Review Romans 12 and 1 Corinthians 13 to see what God says love means.

Day 1
1. Who had to make a choice to love?
2. What was gained and what was lost because of the choice?
3. Have there been times in your life when you have been asked to love like this?

Day 2
1. Both ladies chose to love. How did each show her love?
2. Why did Jesus say one was better than the other?
3. What is our motivation for choosing to love?

Day 3
1. What created the bond between Jonathan and David?
2. Is there a bond in your life that has been created out of similar circumstances?
3. In what ways can you help someone who is just starting on the path that you are already on?

Day 4
1. What types of people did Jesus choose to love?
2. What did it cost Jesus to love on these people?
3. How did Jesus's choice to love change these people?
4. What does it cost you to love people that others don't?

Day 5
1. Which person in this week did you relate to the most? Why?
2. Is there another person in the Bible who made this same choice to love?
3. Is there a person in your life that God is calling you to love in spite of your feelings? How will you take steps to do this?
4. How can you draw strength from the people in the Bible to help you in your choice to love?

The Choice to Love

But anyone who does not love does not know
God, for God is love. –1 JOHN 4:8 NLT

A grandmother and a little girl whose face was sprinkled with bright red freckles spent the day at the zoo. The children were waiting in line to get their cheeks painted by a local artist who was decorating them with tiger paws.

"You've got so many freckles, there's no place to paint!" a boy in the line cried.

Embarrassed, the little girl dropped her head. Her grandmother knelt down next to her.

"I love your freckles," she said.

"Not me," the girl replied.

"Well, when I was a little girl, I always wanted freckles." The grandmother traced her finger across the child's cheek. "Freckles are beautiful!"

The girl looked up. "Really?"

"Of course," said the grandmother. "Why, just name me one thing that's prettier than freckles."

The little girl peered into the old woman's smiling face. "Wrinkles," she answered softly.

[Unknown]

> Love is a choice to see people as God sees them.

Love is a choice to see people as God sees them. Love is a choice that recognizes all of us have faults. It's a choice to show Christ's love to others, regardless of faults or differences. God calls us to love because He is love. True representatives of Christ are called to love others and to love Him. What does love look like? What does love mean?

Read Romans 12:9–21 and 1 Corinthians 13:1–13. List the adjectives that describe what love means. Then, with your list in mind, dig deep each day into the lives of people in the Bible who had to make the choice to love, even when they might have felt someone didn't deserve it.

Romans 12:9-21	1 Corinthians 13:1-13

Day 1: The Father's Choice to Love

Scripture: Luke 15:11–32

He was lost and is found.
LUKE 15:32 NIV

Luke tells the story of three men who loved deeply—one son who loved only himself; another son who loved others conditionally; and the father who loved unconditionally and selflessly. The story of a father and his two sons is woven together with many threads of love. The youngest son's desire for worldly possessions and titles revealed his selfish love. His fleshly desires drove his thoughts and his choices. His love was selfish, and his choices followed what he thought would satisfy him, without regard to the consequences following. Eventually, the consequences did come, but fortunately his final choices allowed him to experience love in a way he never knew.

The oldest son was also selfish. His pride was revealed through his selfish love. He took pride in himself for doing what was right. While his actions were righteous, his heart was not. Our actions eventually expose the purity of our heart. This son loved his father, but his love was conditional. He was jealous of his brother and unwilling to love and forgive. The eldest brother forfeited the love, forgiveness, and grace that the father was offering. He chose to compare one sin against the other instead of choosing to offer love, grace, and mercy regardless of worthiness.

1. What may have prompted the younger son to leave home?

_____

_____

_____

The father loved his sons from the beginning and would love them forever. The younger son eventually chose to accept the love and forgiveness of his father, and their relationship was restored.

The eldest son chose to love himself, and therefore blocked the growth of any relationship with his father.

The father loved his sons unconditionally. He loved the youngest enough to let him go; he loved him enough to watch for his return; and he loved him enough to forgive and accept him just because he was his. The father's love represents the love offered to us from our heavenly Father. This unconditional love is available to us even though we mess up on all levels—some not as deep, others deeper. Our Father is not just *waiting* for us, He's *watching* for us. He is not standing there with arms crossed, waiting to hear the appropriate thing from us. He is standing there with open arms, ready to fill every hole in our heart. Holes of loneliness, disappointment, and unworthiness Satan attempts to pry open are intended to be filled by God and God alone.

Luke 15:17 tells us the younger son "came to his senses," and that opened doors for things to change and life to be different.

2. What changed in verses 15 through 21 that made the younger son come home?

_____

_____

_____

> The Father's love is a model for us.
>
> The son's love is often a reflection of us.

Through the circumstances of his life, the younger son gained an understanding and gratefulness he had never known. In Luke 15:21, the son finally recognized he had misplaced his love. His repentant heart sent him home, and he made the choice to love his father and God no matter the circumstances—even if that means he had to remain a servant. But the father's love shifted the son's focus from his own feelings and onto the grace, mercy, acceptance, and love of his father. Each one of us will love and worship someone or something. We were made to love in Christ's likeness. We must choose very carefully what or to whom we give our hearts.

The younger son made the choice to return, not knowing how his father would respond. Now think about the way the father welcomed his son. The son returned, his head hung low, very low. But when the father saw him, he ran to meet and hug his son. When you hug and are being hugged, your face points upward— upward to the Father, upward to reconciliation, and upward to forgiveness.

When a child comes to an adult and is sad, the adult might respond by putting a hand under the child's chin and raising up their head. The adult's action tells the child that they are valued; they alone have the adult's attention.

3. What almost kept the son from returning?

_____

_____

_____

When we stop to think about it, we begin to realize that God loves us just like the father in the story. He watches for our attention and desires our heart. He is the missing part who will complete us. This son realized he had choices. While some things were choices he made, like taking the money; others were choices made for him, like suffering because of the famine that caused his final destitute state. How he responded was his choice in every situation. He chose to seek the father in the end. He chose what was best. He received the forgiveness he sought—and so much more. The father had always loved him unconditionally, but now the son was at a place where he could see the love and receive it. The father lavished the son with the finest of things celebrating his return.

We get to choose our response to every situation.

As my sister likes to say, "God showed up and showed off!" He is waiting to give us His blessings—and they will always far surpass what we can imagine.

4. *What issues do you think the son dealt with even after returning and accepting all the lavish gifts from his father?*

_____

_____

_____

5. *What issues do you think the older brother struggled with?*

_____

_____

_____

6. *Why do you think it was hard for the older brother to love and forgive the younger?*

_____

_____

_____

Love is a choice. It's a selfless act choosing to put someone else's needs and wants before our own needs and desires. It's a choice. We all want to feel loved, but we can be quick to judge who should receive our love.

7. *Have you ever felt like it was an injustice for someone who has not made good choices to receive a blessing you felt they didn't deserve? If so, how?*

_____

_____

_____

8. *How do you choose to love someone in this situation?*

_____

_____

_____

9. *To which character of this story do you relate the most—the son who left home, the one who stayed home, or the father who always loved and always forgave, who waited on his wayward son to return home? Which one characterizes your life circumstances?*

_____

_____

_____

Scripture: Luke 10:38–42

You are worried and upset about many things.
Only one thing is important.
LUKE 10:41–42 NCV

Both Mary and Martha had very close relationships with Jesus. They loved Him dearly. This story is just a snapshot of their lives—it's not the first time they met Jesus. Jesus was very close to them and their brother Lazarus. In fact, the shortest verse in the Bible, "Jesus wept," reflects Jesus weeping over Lazarus's death. However, in this snapshot, Jesus has come to have dinner at their home. Mary's response was to sit at His feet and to pour the finest oils on His feet. For Mary, nothing mattered more than being with Jesus at that moment. She was not concerned with the house being cleaned or the dinner ready; she only wanted time with her Savior.

1. What blessings did Mary receive because she chose to give up an activity?

_____

_____

_____

Martha also loved Jesus. She wanted to put forth her best for Him. She was concerned that the house would look good and that the food would be magnificent. She wanted everything to be perfect for her Savior. There is no lack of love or respect for Jesus in Martha's response. She also wanted to give Him her absolute best. However, if this is true, why did Jesus say that Mary had made the better, more important choice?

Jesus was driving home a lesson we struggle with today. Have you ever had a dinner party and realized after the fact that you had been so busy being the "hostess with the most-est" that you didn't have a single conversation with anyone? Martha was an incredible hostess, but she was missing out enjoying the people. She was missing her blessing.

2. What blessings did Martha give up because of her service?

_____

_____

_____

> *Our best will never be enough to make us right with God.*

Jesus had another point to teach them: Our best will never be enough to make us right with God. We can never be righteous enough, never clean enough, never perfect enough to measure up to God. That is why He sent us Jesus. Mary did not concern herself with anything but Jesus. All she had was all she needed—Jesus. No matter how hard she tried, Martha could never make herself or her deeds good enough for God. All she needed was Jesus, not all the works (and the exhaustion that goes with it), to look good for Jesus. All Jesus wanted was her attention!

3. Name three ways your life looks like Martha?

_____

_____

_____

4. Name three ways your life looks like Mary?

_____

_____

_____

5. What areas or activities do we need to give up to be able to live a life like Mary?

_____

_____

_____

6. What blessings will we forfeit if we continue to live like Martha?

_____

_____

_____

7. *How do you show Jesus you love Him? Do you perform for Him, or do you have a heart that wants to get to know Him?*

_____

_____

_____

Day 3: Jonathan's Choice to Love

Scripture: 1 Samuel 18:1–4 and 19:1–7

Jonathan made a covenant with David
because he loved him as himself.
1 SAMUEL 18:3

Jonathan was the son of King Saul. He was also best friends with David, God's chosen replacement for Saul's throne. Saul, Jonathan, and David had each found the age of fifteen to be an important year in their lives. Saul was around fifteen when Jonathan was born. Jonathan was around fifteen when he defeated the Philistines. David was about fifteen when he defeated Goliath and was subsequently anointed king. The calling on their lives and the role in the line of power that they each played enabled them to relate to the life experiences each would go through. Jonathan and David shared many experiences that bonded them quickly. Their age, the battles fought, and their loyalty and love for Saul bonded their souls. Jonathan and David formed a very special relationship—one that Proverbs 18:24 would describe as "a friend who sticks closer than a brother." They understood each other's perspective, feelings that surrounded their individual circumstances, and the background of their responses.

1. How well do we know Jonathan? List three or four redeeming qualities of Jonathan.

_____

_____

_____

2. Name two ways Jonathan and David were alike?

_____

_____

_____

Jonathan's father, King Saul, was a very jealous man who ultimately wanted to kill David. Jonathan was able to help guide, support, encourage, and protect David. Jonathan was put in the middle between two people whom he loved. Jonathan faced betraying his father or losing his friend. He had to make a hard choice, but he chose what he knew to be true and right. The choice was not easy, and it cost him his relationship with his father and his place on the throne, but it was right. Jonathan followed God's instruction, for he knew the hand of God was on David. Jonathan made the difficult choice to go with God.

3. What hard choices did Jonathan have to consider and eventually make?

_____

_____

_____

4. How did Jonathan show love to David?

_____

_____

_____

There is a love that comes from the bond between two people who have experienced similar experiences. Whether you share similar feelings, emotions, facts, or situations involved, helping someone through what God has already helped you through is a powerful act of love. Have you ever had the blessing of walking beside someone who was going through an experience similar to your own? Walking alongside that person allows you to see the circumstances through different lenses. When you choose to allow God to use you in someone else's situation, God will allow you to see Him in the midst of the struggle.

Countless times I have chosen to step back from my emotions in a situation, and that is when I was able to see more clearly how God had been working all along. There are times in our struggles of rejection, loss, hurt, and pain when we trust but don't feel like we see God. Emotions alter our thought process. When we choose to walk beside someone and share the faith and trust that carried us through our struggles, we begin to see God moving in our situation.

Seeing God's hand is a step in the healing process, but it's also a step in deepening your relationship with Him. Look for people around you who might need you to walk beside them. Sometimes God places people in our lives to help us as much as we help them.

5. *What ways can you show love to someone by walking beside them in a path that you have already walked?*

_____

_____

_____

6. *In what ways have you been able to see God's hand in your life while helping someone else in his or her journey?*

_____

_____

_____

Day 4: Jesus's Choice to Love

Scripture: Luke 23:32–43;
Mark 6:30–44; Luke 22:1–6

*"Come with me by yourselves to a quiet place
and get some rest."*
Mark 6:31 (NIV)

Jesus showed us the real meaning of love by saving us. Humankind had missed the boat—we strayed from the love God created and wanted us to experience. Our love was a selfish love, one that was all about our gain, not God's. Jesus came to set the standard and measurement right. Jesus was countercultural in many ways, and the people that He chose to love provided a clear example of that fact.

We can see how Jesus loved His disciples. He called each one intentionally knowing they would be entrusted to carry on His mission after He was gone. He lived daily with them. He talked them down when they were angry, and He loved on them when they were lonely or missed their families. He provided for them and five thousand others when their fears of inadequacy were very real. He consistently told and retold them of what was coming. Even though they did not get it, He loved them enough to never give up but continued to invest in each of their lives.

*Jesus loves
us enough to
NEVER give
up on us.*

1. What are some struggles you have with those who you continually invest in?

_____

_____

_____

Jesus loved Judas. He kept him close even though He knew what choice Judas would make. He loved him. Judas betrayed Jesus to the high priest and temple authorities, but he also betrayed the friendship, investment, and love that Jesus had so freely given. Judas chose his way instead of God's way. However, Jesus still loved him.

2. *In what ways do you see Jesus choosing to love people even when they reject, fail, or let Him down?*

_____

_____

_____

For a while, those closest to Jesus, including his own family, didn't recognize who He was and what He was here to do. Initially, His own brothers did not even believe He was the Son of God.

3. *How do you think this made Jesus feel?*

_____

_____

_____

4. *What would have been the biggest struggles with His family?*

_____

_____

_____

5. *What choice did Jesus have to make, despite His feelings involving His family?*

_____

_____

_____

Jesus endured struggles like these and we are guaranteed to experience the same conflicts in life. The Bible doesn't say too much about Jesus and His family issues, but we do get to see the result of Jesus loving them even when they didn't believe in Him.

6. *What are some struggles you have with your own family?*

_____

_____

_____

7. *In what ways can choosing to love change you?*

_____

_____

_____

Day 5: What Does Love Mean for Me?

Scripture: Romans 12 and 1 Corinthians 13

"And now these three remain: faith, hope and love.
But the greatest of these is love."
1 CORINTHIANS 13:13 (NIV)

Choosing to love is hard at times. As we looked back this week at people who were faced with that decision, we see the blessings of choosing to love. Our value is found in Christ, and that has nothing to do with actions. Choosing to love doesn't validate the actions of others; it validates their value in Christ. We have seen how Jesus loved the unlovable and how He changed lives by choosing to love. We are given the same opportunity and command, but it's up to us to make the choice.

Choosing to love doesn't validate the actions of others, it validates their value in Christ.

1. Who is God asking you to choose to love?

_____

_____

_____

2. Is it hard for you to love or be loved by this person? Why?

_____

_____

_____

3. What lesson could you learn through your choice to love?

_____

_____

_____

4. *What might be the joys that come because of that choice? What might be the struggles?*

_____

_____

_____

5. *How does your choice reflect your heart?*

_____

_____

_____

6. *If you can't choose to love them now, will you choose to pray about the situation and to pray for them?*

_____

_____

_____

Lord, forgive us for sitting in Your seat of judgment. You set the standard, not us. Please help us to love each other the way You love us.

The Choice To Obey

Group Discussion Questions

Be prepared to answer these questions with your group next week.

1. *Which person in the Bible did you relate to the most this week?*

_____

_____

_____

_____

_____

_____

2. *Is there another person in the Bible who made this same choice? Who?*

_____

_____

_____

_____

_____

_____

3. *How do their circumstances relate to yours?*

_____

_____

_____

_____

_____

_____

4. *What changes will you make in your life by choosing to love?*

_____

_____

_____

_____

_____

_____

WEEK 2: OBEY

Leader's Questions for Week Two: The Choice to Obey
Review 2 John 1:6 to see what God says about choosing to obey.

Day 1
1. What lessons did Noah learn through his obedience?
2. What consequences would have come if Noah's obedience was delayed?
3. What blessings came to Noah because of his obedience?

Day 2
1. What choice did God ask Moses to make?
2. How did God bless Moses because of his obedience?
3. What blessing, if any, did Moses lose because of his excuses?

Day 3
1. All of Joseph's directions came to him in his dreams. Why do you think he was so willing to act immediately and without question?
2. What blessing did Joseph receive because of his obedience?
3. Joseph's legacy was his obedience to God. What do you want your legacy to be?

Day 4
1. Who did Jesus choose to obey?
2. What did it cost Jesus to obey?
3. What did Jesus gain and accomplish by choosing to obey?

Day 5
1. What person did you relate most to this week?
2. In what area of your life do you need to make a choice to obey?
3. What encouragement can you gain from others' choices to obey?

The Choice to Obey

The word *obey* has quite a negative connotation for us today. It
wasn't long ago when traditional wedding vows even included
this word, but most ceremonies now omit it. We don't want to
obey anyone anymore. We want to be our own authority in our
own lives. Too often, we allow our feelings at the moment to rule
our daily lives. Jeremiah 17:9 warns us that the heart is deceitful;
the "heart" here refers to our feelings. We eat, shop, talk, go to
church, and join groups based on our feelings. If we *don't* feel like
it, we *don't* do it. If we *do* feel like it, we *do* it.

*Obedience
is doing
what is right
regardless
of our
feelings.*

Be careful not to confuse feelings with obedience. God tells us
that obedience is an action. Obedience is doing what is right
regardless of our feelings. Look back at our scripture for the
week—the word *walk* is used prior to *obedience*. Walk is a verb,
and a verb is an action word. It has nothing to do with feelings.
We cannot always choose our feelings, but we can choose what we
do with them—our actions.

My father loved to play golf. When he first started playing, a
friend walked beside him and showed him how to stand in order
to achieve the desired results. The man said, "Stand this way and
swing this direction." Dad looked at him and said, "But that
doesn't feel right." The man replied, "So, do it till it feels right."

You do what you know to be right and let the feelings come later.

This was a huge life lesson. Our feelings must not drive our actions. Our actions must reflect our obedience.

The people we will study this week chose obedience in spite of their feelings. Their obedience allowed God to show up in mighty ways. Their obedience impacted their day and their future as well. Just as we read their stories, they impact us thousands of years later. If we choose to obey, imagine the impact our choices might have, not only for us, but also for our children and the future generations who will read and hear of our stories.

Day 1: Noah's Choice to Obey

Scripture: Genesis 7–8

Noah did everything just as God commanded him.
GENESIS 6:22

At first glance, we usually see this story as one of God's judgments. At this time God decided to destroy the entire earth along with all the people on it through a great flood. The people had chosen to turn completely away from God—all that is, except one man, Noah, and his family. Noah chose God. It couldn't have been easy for Noah, being scoffed and laughed at every day. The Bible says he was the only righteous man, so he obviously didn't have a support group to help him stay strong. His choices were his choices alone, and his obedience resulted in a ride with the Lord that he could never have imagined. Through his act of obedience, Noah experienced more and more of who God was.

True obedience allows us to experience more of who God is.

The real story here is Noah's choice to obey. God asked Noah to build an ark. I can't imagine what Noah thought. Based on Genesis 2:5–6, until that point, rain had never fallen from the sky. The ground was watered from a mist. So God asked Noah to do something he had never heard of, to protect him from something he had never experienced. This required Noah's immediate and continual obedience in order to protect him from what would eventually come. While the Bible's account of this story is short, it took years for the story to be complete. Bible scholars estimate that it took Noah between seventy-five and one hundred and twenty years to build the ark. I don't think anyone of us can say we persevered and worked at one task for that many years. A great team encouraging us would be necessary, but Noah and his family were alone in their endeavor. The people thought Noah was crazy, but nonetheless, Noah tried to convince them to turn back to God. God is a God of many chances, and He continually

God's timing is ALWAYS perfect

seeks us; as Noah continually witnessed to others around him. I doubt Noah felt like giving them any more chances.

1. What would obedience cost Noah and his family?

_____

_____

_____

2. What aspects of life would change for Noah and his family because of his obedience?

_____

_____

_____

3. What feeling was associated with the call to obey?

_____

_____

_____

Another part of the story is God's provision for the faithful. He provided for those He entrusted to be Christlike in the midst of adversity. They were tested, and they passed. They were used to further God's creation, and He provided exactly what they needed. Can you imagine trying to figure out how to build an ark? Not knowing how big it should be or what would be inside? Or how much of which supplies to bring? God provided every detail that was needed, and Noah responded in full faith.

4. What did God ask of Noah?

_____

_____

_____

God's perfect timing is another important element of this story. God controlled everything from the beginning of the flood when the waters would recede, to the time the dove would find dry land. God told Noah at His appointed time what to build. He brought the animals at His appointed time, so that they would be safe when the rain began. There was a reason and a purpose in God's perfect timing of every detail. Noah had full faith God would deliver him and his family from the ark one day. Genesis 8:1 says that the Lord "sent a wind over the earth, and the waters receded." I wonder what it must have been like to feel a wind strong enough to evaporate that much water. I imagine it must have been a little scary, if not terrifying.

5. *What fears did Noah have to overcome?*

_____

_____

_____

For the end result to happen, there had to be wind. Think about wind for a moment with me. Wind can be refreshing on a hot summer day. Wind can chap your face when you are outside in the cold. Wind can tear a home apart during a tornado. There are many kinds of "wind" in our lives that must come before the calm can result. We can see the "why" in this story, but so many times in our lives, the why is never seen. Without the wind, the water would not have dried and there would not have been dry land. Without the dry land, there would have been no exit, nor would there have been a new start for humanity. I wonder if the thought ever crossed their minds that they might die in the wind? I wonder if they ever questioned if God had brought them this far to let them die? *There will be many times in life where the wind will blow very hard and we will wonder whether we can stand in the midst of it—but God has always been and will always be faithful.* Even if the wind seems too strong to stand against and we fall down, it will eventually stop, and God will be there to stand us up and set us down at His perfect appointed time and place.

6. *What did Noah have to give up in order to do what God called him to do?*

_____

_____

_____

God has always been and will always be faithful.

7. How did his choice affect his family and friends?

_____

_____

_____

8. What lesson can we learn through Noah's obedience?

_____

_____

_____

9. How did Noah's choice reflect his heart?

_____

_____

_____

10. Is there something God is asking of you that requires trust on your part?

_____

_____

_____

11. In what ways can you relate to Noah's stepping out in faith?

_____

_____

_____

Day 2: Moses's Choice to (kinda) Obey

Scripture: Exodus 4

"Now go; I will help you speak and
will teach you what to say."
EXODUS 4:12 (NIV)

Summarize in your own words what Exodus 4 tells us:

_____
_____
_____
_____
_____
_____
_____
_____

Moses was given direct steps to take with God by his side, and yet he questioned everything God said. He had a response for every directive. God eventually lost patience with Moses, and His wrath burned against him. God still asked Moses to go, but Aaron received the blessing and Moses would now assist. God showed Moses many miracles that night, but Moses still questioned how the mission would be accomplished.

1. How did God speak or call Moses?

_____
_____
_____

2. What was God asking of Moses?

_____
_____
_____

Excuses keep our focus on what <u>WE</u> can do instead of what <u>GOD</u> can do.

3. What would it cost Moses to obey?

_____

_____

_____

_____

If you are a parent or if you remember being a child, you know bedtime can be a rough experience. The nightly routine can sometimes run in circles. You say good night, and then the child gets up again—she needs water. You say good night, and then she gets up again—she needs a tissue. You say good night, and then she gets up again—she forgot to pack her snack. The routine with its frustration and excuses continues until patience is lost and future blessings are taken away. If only she had done what was asked the first time, without arguing and without excuse, the mission would have been accomplished and she would have had the blessing of praise in the morning and a good night's sleep. I wonder if God felt like He was dealing with a child that night. I wonder if He might feel that way toward us when He asks us to do something and we give Him excuses. I wonder how many blessings we have missed because we didn't choose immediate obedience.

Moses responded with excuses of unworthiness, inadequacy, and fear. These feelings are not holy excuses; they are selfish ones. These feelings become excuses that keep us from receiving the blessing because our feelings—which tend to drive our actions— are all about us. *The excuses keep the focus on what **we** can do instead of what **God** can do.* He wants to bless us and use us.

4. What fears would Moses have to overcome to be obedient?

_____

_____

_____

5. What physical, spiritual, and emotional ways did God provide for Moses?

_____

_____

_____

6. *Why did God get angry with Moses?*

_____

_____

_____

7. *What lessons can we learn from Moses and the burning bush?*

_____

_____

_____

8. *Have you ever responded to a calling with excuses?*

_____

_____

_____

9. *Name a time when God called you to do something that you felt was out of your comfort zone or that you felt ill-equipped to do. What was your response? What did it cost you?*

_____

_____

_____

_____

Day 3: Joseph's Choice to Obey

Scripture: Matthew 1:18–24;
Matthew 2:13–14; and Luke 2:33–51

*When Joseph woke up, he did what the angel of the
Lord had commanded him.*
MATTHEW 1:24

Jesus's earthly father Joseph is most often referred to as Mary's husband. He does not hold a prominent role in much of the Bible; however his choices regarding his role were crucial. God chose Joseph because He knew his heart and He knew Joseph would choose to obey without question. Joseph's choice to obey would help to facilitate the fulfillment of the prophecy of the coming Messiah. That's pretty huge for such a small role!

1. What do we know about Joseph?

_____

_____

_____

2. What do Joseph's actions tell us about his character?

_____

_____

_____

The Bible doesn't talk about Joseph's religious lifestyle or beliefs; however, we do know that angels spoke to Joseph three different times, and without question Joseph woke up and immediately obeyed their instruction. His faith in God must have been strong to respond the way he did. Joseph and Mary were pledged to be married. A pledge to be married in that day required a certificate of divorce to break. According to the law, Mary would face public disgrace and even stoning if people found out she was pregnant. Joseph knew this and wanted to protect her, so he prepared to quietly divorce her. Then an angel spoke to him in a dream and told Joseph not to do it, but to take her home as his wife. Joseph obeyed. (Matthew 1:18-24)

3. *In accordance with the culture, what were some costs that Joseph faced because of his obedience to take Mary as his wife and to raise the Son of God?*

_____

_____

_____

4. *Joseph chose to trust God and to trust Mary. In what ways would that have been very hard? (See Matthew 1:19.)*

_____

_____

_____

After Jesus was born in Bethlehem, another angel came to Joseph in a dream. He told Joseph to take Mary and Jesus and go immediately to Egypt in order to save their lives. Joseph obeyed. And in yet another dream, an angel appeared to Joseph and told him to alter his plans once more and return to Nazareth because of a change in rulers. Again, Joseph obeyed. (Matthew 2:13-14)

5. *Joseph was marrying a woman who was carrying a baby who was the Son of God. What kind of role do you think Joseph would play in Mary and Jesus' life?*

_____

_____

_____

Joseph's choice to obey didn't come without a cost. The culture at this time was patriarchal, and the family name was carried on through the father's line (Matthew 1:1–16). Each census in each country was counted by the father's birthplace (Luke 2:4). A person's value during this time came from the father's line. If this was the culture at the time of Jesus' birth, what do you think Joseph might have felt and/or chosen to give up in order to be the "earthly father" (essentially, a stepfather) to the Son of God? Do you think Joseph ever felt like a stepfather (Luke 2:49)? Do you think he ever wondered what his exact role was in Jesus' life? Do you think there was ever a struggle between him and Mary over who was the authority figure in their marriage or as parents?

6. *What personal rights do you think Joseph might have put aside in order to be obedient to God's calling? Look at Luke 2:49.*

_____

_____

_____

7. *What are some situations today that would require Joseph's type of obedience?*

_____

_____

_____

There are a lot of choices being made everyday concerning relationships and babies. The burden of the choice is real, and the judgment was a real fear for Joseph, but he obeyed in his new role. Was the path different from his dream? Absolutely!

Joseph's legacy was his choice to obey God.

Joseph heard from God, and he obeyed. He didn't rationalize the dreams or the situation, nor did he excuse it— he simply obeyed. Joseph's feelings came second to the calling on his life. ***Joseph's blessing for his obedience was Jesus Christ.*** His legacy was his choice to obey God.

8. *What do you want your legacy to be?*

_____

_____

_____

Day 4: Jesus's Choice to Obey

Scripture: Luke 2:41–52

Then {Jesus} went down to Nazareth with them
and was obedient to {his parents}.
LUKE 2:51

The Bible tells us that Jesus was the Son of God (Mark 14:60–64; John 1:1, 14). Jesus was also born to Mary and was human just like we are (Luke 1:26–38). Jesus had the same struggles that we do, and He had choices to make just like we do. When He was little, He had to obey His parents. When Jesus was twelve, Mary and Joseph took their family to Jerusalem for the Passover festival just like they did every year. This time, when they headed home, Jesus stayed behind in the temple without telling his mom. For three days, His family searched for Him. When they found Him, they questioned Him as to why He had done this? He explained that he was in His Father's house, but obeyed and returned home with his parents.

Have you ever lost a child in a store? It's a terrifying experience. I am sure Mary panicked, wondering how she could have lost the Son of God. We have pressure today to be good parents; I can imagine the pressure on Mary was even more so. The passage ends with Jesus returned safely to his family. Jesus' response quickly reminded Mary of who Jesus was and what His purpose was for being in this world.

In John 2:1-11, we find another example of Jesus choosing to obey His mother, this time during a wedding they attended. Mary tells Jesus that the wine had run out. "Why do you involve me? My time has not yet come," Jesus responds. But Mary turns to the servants and says, "Do whatever He tells you." I am sure we can relate to this. I know my mom urged me to do some things that I resisted, but later realized I just needed to obey.

I did have a choice to obey, and so did Jesus. He may not have been comfortable or felt the timing was right, but He obeyed His mother.

1. Do you think Jesus always felt like obeying?

_____

_____

_____

> Jesus's ultimate obedience was His choice to go to the cross.

Jesus also chose to obey God. When Jesus went into the desert, He was tempted greatly by Satan when He was at His weakest point. Physically and emotionally, Jesus was empty—He had been in the desert for forty days without food and water—but spiritually He was strong, and He chose to lean on the words of God when He had nothing else.

2. What did Jesus give up to obey?

_____

_____

_____

Jesus's ultimate obedience was His choice to go to the cross. When Jesus prayed in the garden of Gethsemane, He asked, "Father, if you are willing, take this cup from me, yet not my will, but yours be done" (Luke 22:42). Jesus knew what was ahead and could have chosen to forego the cross, but He was obedient to what He knew was right and God's will, even when His feelings didn't match up.

3. What are some areas in which Jesus had to surrender His will?

_____

_____

_____

4. What did Jesus gain by His obedience?

_____

_____

_____

True obedience is to surrender your will and your personal rights to do what God asks.

5. *What are some areas in which you need to surrender your will and your rights?*

_____

_____

_____

6. *What could you gain by your obedience? What could you lose?*

_____

_____

_____

7. *What or who do our actions ultimately reflect? Who are we choosing to honor and obey? How should this change our response to situations?*

_____

_____

_____

Day 5: What Does Obedience Mean for Me?

As obedient children, do not conform to the evil desires
you had when you lived in ignorance.
I PETER 1:14 NIV

This week, we have looked at people who chose to surrender their rights and their desires to do what was right in the eyes of God. Sometimes what we are doing is not wrong, it's just not the path that God wants us to take. His will for our lives may be different than the activities and plans that we have. We may not even realize in the busyness of our lives that God is calling us to change course. We may not realize that we are disobeying until we take the time to hear Him. We have a choice in everything we do—every activity, every response, and every action. Sometimes choosing to obey may be easy; other times obeying may be the hardest choice we ever have to make.

1. In which areas of life do you need to choose to obey God?

_____
_____
_____

2. Who are you currently choosing to obey?

_____
_____
_____

3. What encouragement or strength can you gain from others who have made the hard choice to obey?

_____
_____
_____

4. *Are there some areas in your life that you are choosing NOT to obey or choosing to ignore God?*

_____

_____

_____

5. *What areas of your life do you need to surrender so that you can obey what God is asking of you?*

_____

_____

_____

Lord, forgive us for being a stiff-necked people. You have so many blessings You want to give us, but in our disobedience, we miss out on so much. Most of all we miss You. We miss out on the journey of life with You. Help us to see the areas that we neglect and in our pride keep from You, so that we may willingly surrender and obey Your commands.

The Choice to Forgive

Group Discussion Questions

Be prepared to answer these questions with your group next week.

1. *Which person in the Bible did you relate to the most this week?*

_____

_____

_____

_____

_____

_____

2. *Is there another person in the Bible who made this same choice? Who?*

_____

_____

_____

_____

_____

_____

3. *How do their circumstances relate to yours?*

_____

_____

_____

_____

_____

_____

4. *What changes will you make in your life by choosing to love?*

_____

_____

_____

_____

_____

_____

WEEK 3: THE CHOICE TO FORGIVE

Review Colossians 3:12–13 (NLT) to see what God says about forgiveness.

Day 1
1. Why did Jonah choose to run?
2. What was his biggest issue with the Ninevites?
3. What lesson did God want to teach Jonah?

Day 2
1. Why did Hosea keep going after Gomer?
2. Do you relate to or resemble Gomer in any way?
3. What does forgiveness look like in your life?

Day 3
1. Why do you think Joseph chose to forgive his brothers?
2. What blessings came because of Joseph's choices?
3. What did Joseph have to be willing to give up in order to forgive?

Day 4
1. Name some people to whom Jesus offered forgiveness?
2. How did Jesus's choice to forgive people impact those around Him?
3. When does Jesus tell us that forgiveness is appropriate?
4. In what areas and in what circumstances are we called to forgive like Jesus does?

Day 5
1. Which person did you relate to most this week?
2. What area in your life do you need to choose to forgive?
3. What strength can you gain from others' choice to forgive?

The Choice to Forgive

Scripture for the Week

Clothe yourselves with tenderhearted mercy, kindness, humility, gentleness, and patience. Make allowance for each other's faults, and forgive anyone who offends you. Remember, the Lord forgave you, so you must forgive others. —COLOSSIANS 3:12–13 NLT

What makes forgiveness such a hard choice? Why do so many of us struggle with offering forgiveness? Choosing to forgive in this world often seems like we are validating the act; that in some way, we are saying what happened is okay. Forgiveness can be seen as a sign of weakness or a sign of acceptance. The world says we should seek revenge because we were wronged. The world says we did not deserve what happened, and someone has to pay. These observations and definitions are the world's standards. So often forgiveness in this world is conditional. We think, *I'll forgive as long as you don't hurt me again.* However, as soon as a new offense is committed, we mix everything into the same pile again and the forgiveness extended is taken back. Our view of forgiveness is clouded by our selfishness.

This is not the forgiveness God asks us to choose. The forgiveness God offers and He asks us to choose, frees us. The Greek word *aphiemi* means to "leave, pardon, remit, cancel, repented or abandon." Forgiveness allows us to put the baggage down and to look forward to the blessings that God promises He will make out of our rubble. God's entire purpose of sending His one and only Son was to forgive. God knew the only way to reconcile relationships, primarily ours with Him is to place forgiveness at the foundation.

What does true forgiveness look like? True forgiveness is putting others before yourself. It's allowing God to sit in His rightful seat and to be the standard and the judge. Forgiveness is looking past the action to see the person, learning to see them through God's eyes. Forgiveness understands that the other person's value does not rest in how we view them, but in how Christ views them. Christ gave His life so that we might find forgiveness from our sin. It is this forgiveness that gives each of us the opportunity to reconcile our own relationship with God. Christ died for everyone. Our value is only found in Him.

Corrie ten Boom, in her book, *Reflections of God's Glory*[1] wrote,

> In Africa, a man came to a meeting with bandaged hands. I asked him how he had been injured. He said, "My neighbor's straw roof was on fire; I helped him to put it out, and that's how my hands were burned." Later I heard the whole story. The neighbor hated him and had set his roof on fire while his wife and children were asleep in the hut. They were in great danger. Fortunately, he was able to put out the fire in his house on time. But sparks flew over to the roof of the man who had set the house on fire, and his house started to burn. There was no hate in the heart of this Christian; there was love for his enemy, and he did everything he could to put out the fire in his neighbor's house. That is how his own hands were burned.

Throughout this week, we will read about people who had to make a very difficult choice to forgive. They had every worldly reason to hold a grudge and to hate those who had wronged them. Some of them chose forgiveness, and we see the impact of that choice both in their lives and in the life of the person who received the gift. Others gave it and then took it back, and we will see the impact of that as well. Forgiveness is not deserved; it's a gift.

Forgiveness is looking past the action to see the person as God sees them.

Forgiveness is not deserved it's a gift.

50

Forgiveness is a gift that we are given. We are expected to forgive others in return.

Let me remind you as we read through the stories of these people's lives that, just like us, they lived one day and one choice at a time. The goal of this study is to draw strength from seeing the end result of right choices being made. Your story can turn out just as incredible as others, living one day at a time and one choice at a time.

Day 1: Jonah's Choice Not to Forgive

Scripture: Read Jonah 1–4

When God saw what they had done and how they had put a stop to their evil ways, He changed His mind and did not carry out the destruction He had threatened. This change of plans greatly upset Jonah, and he became very angry.
JONAH 3:10–4:1 NLT

God called Jonah to be a vessel to change people's lives, so God could affect their eternity. Jonah did not see any value in these people, and therefore, ran to get far away from them and from God.

1. What was God's initial request of Jonah?

_____

_____

_____

Jonah knew God and worshipped God, so he knew God was "a gracious and compassionate God slow to get angry and filled with unfailing love" (Jonah 4:2 NLT). Jonah wanted all those benefits from God and even praised God while he was in the belly of the fish for being a gracious and compassionate God. Jonah did not, however, want God to forgive the Ninevites for their sins because Jonah deemed them unworthy

2. Why did Jonah hate the Ninevites so much?

_____

_____

_____

Jonah eventually obeyed and went to the people of Nineveh. He was the reason they saw their evil ways and turned back to God.

Jonah wanted to deliver a message of God's wrath which they deserved in Jonah's eyes. He hoped God would destroy them.

3. *What kept Jonah from offering forgiveness even though he had already received it for himself?*

_____

_____

_____

God was going to use this opportunity to show the people of Nineveh His forgiveness, changing their lives and their eternity. Unfortunately, Jonah hardened his heart. The grace and forgiveness Jonah so freely and gratefully accepted in his own time of need did not soften his heart toward others. He was not willing to pass on the gift he'd been given. Jonah died with an unforgiving and bitter spirit.

4. *What blessing did Jonah miss out on because of his bitterness?*

_____

_____

_____

Consider your relationship with God:

5. *Is there something for which God has shown you forgiveness?*

_____

_____

_____

6. *Did you deserve His forgiveness?*

_____

_____

_____

7. *Why did God choose to forgive you?*

_____

_____

_____

Consider your personal life:

8. Is there someone God is calling you to forgive, from whom you are withholding forgiveness?

_____

_____

_____

9. Do they deserve your forgiveness?

_____

_____

_____

10. Why should you choose to forgive them?

_____

_____

_____

11. What blessing could you receive because of your choice?

_____

_____

_____

Day 2: Hosea's Choice to Forgive

Scripture: Hosea 1–3

The Lord said to me, "Go, show your love
to your wife again."
Hosea 3:1

Hosea was a prophet that served God just before the destruction of Israel in 722 BC. He preached to the northern kingdom of Israel and Ephraim. God's plan for Hosea was to allow him to live out what he would preach. His marriage to Gomer, the prostitute, would mirror the relationship between Israel and God. Israel consistently betrayed God, just like Gomer would do to Hosea. God consistently went after His bride and loved her just like Hosea would have to do with Gomer. Hosea's passion as a prophet would come from a place of experience including pain and love. He would experience exactly what God experienced with the Israelites and with us. The interesting picture is that while Gomer is an example of Israel, Israel is an example of us. Israel was great at praising God when things were good. They were also very quick to forget His deliverance and to turn from Him when times were hard. God allowed the Israelites to suffer their own consequences at times. He would use a prophet like Isaiah, Elijah or Hosea to call out their sin and call them to repentance, because his ultimate goal was for ultimate restoration. Hosea's ultimate goal for Gomer was for her unfaithfulness to be acknowledged and for godly disciple to redirect her actions and heart in order to allow for ultimate restoration to follow. Hosea modeled the love and forgiveness that God extends to us.

1. Do you think it was hard for Hosea to marry someone with such great faults?

_____

_____

_____

Faithful Hosea married Gomer, and they had a son together. Then we read that she had a daughter as well—but this daughter was not Hosea's daughter. Gomer then conceived another son, which was also not Hosea's. Time and time again, Hosea took Gomer back after she continually rejected the love he offered. He did not ask anything of her except her love. She desired worldly things and made them her priority. Over and over, she defiled her marriage bed and betrayed her commitment to her husband. Yet every time she left to follow her desires, Hosea went after her, forgave her, and paid another price to bring her home.

2. Why do you think Hosea kept going back to get Gomer?

_____

_____

_____

3. Do you think he was disappointed every time she left?

_____

_____

_____

Did Hosea have the right to leave her? Yes, he had that right, but he chose not to use it. He chose to love her through her faults and her wrong choices because he saw her as redeemable.

4. Do you think Hosea hoped she would change every time he brought her home?

_____

_____

_____

Have you ever met someone who didn't know how to accept love? They usually go from person to person, using them and then discarding them. They are searching for a love that truly values them and gives them purpose and significance, but this can only be found in Christ. It's only when our eyes are fixed on Him that we get the blessing of knowing our true worth. God used Gomer's rejection to teach Hosea a lesson, which would allow him to see the true heart of God.

5. How did Hosea respond when Gomer didn't change?

_____

_____

_____

Just like God, we have the choice to forgive. He chooses to love us and then to forgive us when we choose to love something else. God felt rejection over and over from His chosen people, and now He was allowing Hosea to feel just like He does when we reject Him. As Hosea learned this lesson and walked with God through his sufferings, he was then able to speak from the heart of God to God's people. Hosea is the image of God, the reflection of our heavenly Father, and we reflect the actions of Gomer. We stray over and over from the ways of God. We give away our hearts every time we desire something over God. But just like Hosea, God will never give up on us. He will always actively seek us. Like the shepherd went after one sheep who strayed in Luke 15:4, God will come after us every time.

Our focus in this study is the forgiveness Hosea chose to extend. Gomer did not deserve his forgiveness. Hosea forgave because it was the only way to help restore her to God. He forgave because God asked him to. Forgiveness doesn't validate the sin. Forgiveness acknowledges the value of the person through Christ.

> *Forgiveness doesn't validate the sin, it acknowledges the value of the person through Christ.*

You have to hear me on this, Forgiveness is God's gift to you. You need to accept it and share it. Without forgiveness in your life, your heart can not be freed up to love in any capacity. You are forgiven because Christ paid the price for you to have it. If you don't accept it, then His gift for you of forgiveness and eternal life with Him was in vain. If Christ was willing to die for us, then we must be willing to go after other's who need our forgiveness, again and again, just like Christ does with us. Jesus chose to give up His rights. He chose to forgive when forgiveness wasn't warranted. He chose to see us as redeemable when the world would just use us and cast us aside. Christ will always choose to go get us, because He finds us redeemable.

6. *Is there a broken relationship in your life that would require your forgiveness to heal or continue?*

_____

_____

_____

7. *What is God asking of you in that relationship?*

_____

_____

_____

8. *What rights will you have to set aside in order for you to be an image or reflection of God to them?*

_____

_____

_____

9. *Think of a time when you may have disappointed or hurt someone close to you. How did he or she respond to you? Did he or she choose to forgive you?*

_____

_____

_____

10. *Think of a time when a person closest to you disappointed or hurt you. How did you respond? Did you choose to forgive?*

_____

_____

_____

11. *If we follow God's instructions and Hosea's model, how should we respond the next time we are hurt or disappointed?*

_____

_____

_____

12. How many times are we supposed to forgive someone? (See Matthew 18:22.)

_____

_____

_____

13. What lessons can we learn from the actions that Hosea chose to take to forgive someone who hurt him so badly?

_____

_____

_____

14. What benefit can we gain from offering forgiveness instead of holding onto our rights?

_____

_____

_____

15. What do you do if the person you are supposed to forgive is yourself?

_____

_____

_____

16. Are the rules different because it's you? How does God expect us to respond when we are Gomer?

_____

_____

_____

Day 3: Joseph's Choice to Forgive

Scripture: Genesis 37 and 45:4–6

You intended to harm me, but God intended it all
for good. He brought me to this position so I could
save the lives of many people.
Genesis 50:20

Joseph was the eleventh of twelve boys born to Jacob late in life, and he was his father's favorite child (37:3). He was the son of Jacob's one true love, Rachel. His brothers were very jealous of their relationship. One day, when Joseph was somewhere between seventeen and twenty-five years old, Jacob asked Joseph to check on his brothers while they were tending the sheep. Joseph complied, never expecting the life-altering event which was about to happen. His brothers were mean and envious and decided to sell him as a slave to traders from another country. They told their father that an animal killed him. This seemingly catastrophic event changed Joseph's life dramatically, and many years later, he would have to make a choice of whether to forgive his brothers or hold on to the anger, resentment, and bitterness that eventually comes from choosing not to forgive.

God was already there in every choice and every decision, ready to make something good out of the horrible choices Joseph's brothers had made. Romans 8:28 says, that God "works all things together for good to those who love Him according to His purposes."

There will be times in our lives, too, when things will look bad. But like Joseph, it's possible that those circumstances are intended to set us up for a miraculous encounter with the one true God. Sometimes it's only in the alone, lonely and desperate quiet times we are able to hear from God.

God places the right people at the right time in our lives. This positions us to ultimately receive His blessing. Joseph learned to trust God when life was unfair! He would later find himself at a crossroads regarding forgiveness.

As the years went by and because of his loyalty and faithfulness, Joseph moved up the ranks from prisoner and slave to governor of Egypt. Eventually, there was widespread famine, and Joseph's brothers came to Egypt from nearby Israel to buy food for the family. Joseph and his brothers had not communicated since they sold him. They had no idea if the other was dead or alive. This was the first time Joseph would come face to face with the ones who hurt, deceived, and hated him so much. As we read the story in Genesis 42, we find that Joseph did indeed, struggle with how to treat them. Joseph fought to keep his emotions under control. He had to make a quick choice in his response to his brothers that now stood before him asking for his help.

Our circumstances can set us up for a miraculous encounter with the One True God.

1. *What do you think his brothers were feeling as this Egyptian ruler seemed to know their past? (42:21–22)*

_____

_____

_____

2. *What do you think Joseph was feeling as he turned away and wept? (42:24)*

_____

_____

_____

Joseph positioned himself close to God and then chose to forgive because God had forgiven him.

3. *This was Joseph's time. He was in charge, and he could have his revenge and no one would blame him. What do you think had kept his heart soft throughout all these years? (43:29–30)*

_____

_____

_____

4. *What blessing did Joseph receive through his choice to forgive his brothers? (43:29–30)*

_____

_____

_____

On a scale of one to ten, Joseph's right to hold a grudge was a *ten*! Joseph's brothers sold him into slavery, and then told his father he was dead. Yet, Joseph positioned himself close to God and chose to forgive because God had forgiven him. Joseph knew what it was like to have a close intimate relationship with his earthly father. When the long days and nights no longer provided comfort and love for Joseph, he chose to rely on his heavenly Father to fill every hole in his heart, and God did not let him down!

That's the funny thing about forgiveness—it opens the holes in our heart so that they can be perfectly and completely filled by God. Joseph didn't struggle with forgiving his brothers for long because restoring the relationship with his father was more important than being the judge.

> Forgiveness opens the holes in our heart so it can be perfectly and completely filled by God.

5. *Is there someone close to you (family, friend, or foe) who has hurt you? Is your heart soft or hard toward that person?*

_____

_____

_____

6. *If that person came to you in need, what would be your response?*

_____

_____

_____

7. *What does God want your response to be?*

_____

_____

_____

8. What good have you seen come from forgiveness in your life?

_____

_____

_____

Forgiveness sets us free from the bondage of our rights, feelings, and conditional judgments. It gives us the freedom to love and to be loved; it frees us to enjoy our own unconditional forgiveness from the one true Judge.

Day 4: Jesus's Choice to Forgive

Scripture: John 8:1–11; John 4; Luke 23:39–43

Let any one of you who is without sin be
the first to throw a stone.
JOHN 8:7

Jesus's life shows us exactly what forgiveness looks like. There are many occasions in the Gospels when men wanted to judge and convict, but Jesus intervened with grace and forgiveness. We will look at three different encounters where Jesus chose to offer forgiveness, therefore showing the heart of God. First is a woman who had committed adultery; next is a woman who was living with a man out of wedlock, and lastly is the thief on the cross.

In the first encounter, as told in John 8:1–11, a woman who had committed adultery was brought by the teachers of the law and the Pharisees before Jesus. They challenged Jesus, demanding, "In the Law, Moses commanded us to stone such women. Now what do you say?" Jesus bent down, wrote something in the sand, and then said, "Let anyone of you who is without sin be the first to throw a stone at her." One after another, the men dropped their stones and left. Jesus looked up and asked the woman where everyone was and if anyone had condemned her. She said, "Not one, Lord." And Jesus told her, "Neither do I condemn you; go and sin no more."

1. Why were the leaders and Pharisees so quick to stone a person that was caught in sin?

_____

_____

_____

Jesus' response to forgive and not condemn is powerful, because it shows us the heart of God. The heart of God is all about forgiveness and redemption, not condemnation. According to the law, Jesus would have been right in affirming the people's desire to stone an adulterous woman. God, however, is about redeeming the one who has broken the law. In Romans 8:1, Paul tells us "there is now no condemnation for those who are in Christ Jesus." Jesus' last words to the woman were "go and sin no more."

The measurement tool we all use—the law—allows us to compare and contrast the wrong things we do. We look at the law and see how others measure up to it; we look at our neighbors and see how they measure according to our standards. What we often disregard, however, is how all of us measure according to Christ's standard. Therefore, we never see others the way Christ sees them. Christ looked at that woman through very different lenses than the Pharisees and the teachers used. We, too, should see others as Christ sees them and therefore, treat them just as Christ chose to do.

2. *What was the purpose of Jesus's response to the teachers and Pharisees?*

_____

_____

_____

3. *How did Jesus's choice to forgive impact the woman?*

_____

_____

_____

4. *How do you think Jesus's choice to forgive impacted the people who walked away?*

_____

_____

_____

> Jesus made the choice to forgive because He found us all redeemable.

For our second encounter, let's look at John 4. In this passage, Jesus stopped to rest beside a well while the disciples left him and went into town. A woman came to draw water from the well. She was a Samaritan; Jesus was a Jew. Those two people groups were not suppose to associate with each other. Jesus looked at the woman and knew she was living in sin. He exposed the nature of her sin, yet Jesus, with full knowledge of her life, simply asked her for water from the well. Jesus explained how taking the living water would satisfy her soul and she would never be thirsty again. Jesus' priority was offering her grace and forgiveness. This is how He got her attention and then was able to call out her sin. If Jesus would have walked up and condemned her before telling her about the true living water, then her ears and heart would have been closed. Jesus made a choice to forgive her because she was redeemable in His eyes.

Jesus finds our value in Him, so even while we are in the midst of our sin, we are still offered grace and forgiveness—not because of us, but because of Him.

5. *In what ways do you think the life of that woman changed, both that day and for eternity, because of Jesus' choice to offer forgiveness and grace?*

_____

_____

_____

> God is primarily concerned with the barriers that we place between Him and us.

6. *In what ways do you think the woman's life may have affected the men she had lived with?*

_____

_____

_____

7. *In what areas of your life is Jesus waiting at your well, to refocus your choices and offer grace and forgiveness?*

_____

_____

_____

The third encounter we will study is shown in Luke 23:39–43. Here we see Jesus forgive the thief on the cross. In the last moments of his life, the man who lived a life of sin saw Jesus for who He truly was. In his dying breath, he asked Jesus to remember him in His kingdom. Jesus replied, "Today you will be with me in Paradise." In that moment, the thief's heart discovered the true Savior.

God knows we sin—that's why He sent Jesus to save us. He is not concerned with the hierarchy of sin, which we establish; He is concerned with the barriers we place between Him and us. He is the God of redemption. He chooses to forgive us, even in our last breath.

8. *Jesus forgave someone who had indirectly rejected Him through his actions. What was it that made Jesus welcome him "into His kingdom" that day?*

_____

_____

_____

9. *What lesson do you think Jesus wants us to learn from His example that day?*

_____

_____

_____

10. *In what ways can we apply this example to our lives?*

_____

_____

_____

Day 5: What Does Forgiveness Mean for Me?

Scripture: Matthew 6:14-15

For if you forgive other people when they sin against
you, your heavenly Father will also forgive you.
But if you do not forgive men their sins,
your Father will not forgive your sins.
MATTHEW 6:14-15

Forgiveness is a gift for both the giver and the receiver. It frees both people to become more like Christ. We can only offer true forgiveness when we recognize how much we need it in our own lives. Christ came to forgive us of our sins, therefore we are supposed to forgive those who sin against us.

Consider your relationships and the wrongs doings to others as you answer the following questions.

1. Is there a person in your life whom you have hurt deeply?

_____

_____

_____

2. Has this person chosen to forgive you? Do you deserve to be forgiven?

_____

_____

_____

3. What changes did you make in your life because of their choice to forgive you?

_____

_____

_____

Now consider the relationships and the wrongs done to you as you answer the following questions.

4. *What person in your life has hurt you deeply?*

_____

_____

_____

5. *Have you chosen to forgive them? Did they deserve to be forgiven? Did you tell them?*

_____

_____

_____

6. *Why did you or did you not forgive them?*

_____

_____

_____

7. *Do you know of any changes that were made in their life because of your choice to forgive them?*

_____

_____

_____

8. *What impact did your choice to forgive have on your life?*

_____

_____

_____

Lord, may our eyes be opened to see others as You see them. May we freely offer the same forgiveness that You offer us, so that our lives may help point others to You. May we continually look at our lives and strive to be reflections of Your character in our choices. Thank you for our forgiveness as we fall short daily and thank you for waiting with open arms to restore a right relationship with us. We don't deserve Your gift but we are so thankful that You choose to forgive us. Help us to become more like You as we seek to make choices that are pleasing in Your eyes..

The Choice to Surrender

Group Discussion Questions

Be prepared to answer these questions with your group next week.

1. Which person in the Bible did you relate to the most this week?

_____

_____

_____

_____

_____

_____

2. Is there another person in the Bible who made this same choice? Who?

_____

_____

_____

_____

_____

3. How do their circumstances relate to yours?

_____

_____

_____

_____

_____

4. What changes will you make in your life by choosing to love?

_____

_____

_____

_____

_____

_____

WEEK 4: SURRENDER

Leader's Questions for Week Four: The Choice to Surrender
Review Proverbs 23:26 to see what God says about surrender.

Day 1

1. In what ways was David seeking control?
2. What impact did the control that David sought have on those around him?
3. What result came from David's desire to have control?

Day 2

1. What did Sarah seek to control?
2. What did Sarah lose in her desire to fix things?
3. What should Sarah have done?

Day 3

1. What emotions do you think Mary felt as she realized that her time of authority in Jesus's life was coming to a close?
2. How different would things have looked if Mary hadn't surrendered control of her son?
3. How can you relate to changing roles in relationships?
4. What is the definition of surrender?

Day 4

1. In what areas did Satan try to tempt Jesus?
2. How did Jesus maintain control by submitting to authorities?
3. How did Jesus fight the temptation to control the circumstances?

Day 5

1. Which person did you relate to the most this week?
2. In what areas do you struggle to surrender in your life?
3. How would things look different if you surrendered them to God?
4. Who in your life can you look to for guidance?

The Choice to Surrender

Scripture for the Week

My son, give me your heart, and let
your eyes observe my ways.
PROVERBS 23:26 ESV

Choosing to surrender is very scary for me. I like to feel in control of my life and the things around me. Some tragic things have happened to me at a young age in my life. I knew far to young the pain of grief and loss. It left me feeling helpless and vulnerable. The feeling of not being in control and being a passenger in my own life is terrifying for me. The need for control is directly associated with fear. I don't want to feel the pain, loss, or grief that I have previously known. It hurts. As a result, I found myself attempting to control everything around me in order to keep from having to feel that way again.

As I began to hand this fear over to God, I became aware of Him in new ways. I started to see Him in the details of my past pain. I began to understand that without the pain that my family and I have experienced, I would not know my Lord and Savior as intimately as I do today. As my days (and now years) continue to come and go, I have realized that it was the pain that allowed me to choose to surrender to God. Surrendering my control has allowed me to grow, learn, and rely on the One who truly does have control—not me, but God.

I find myself learning this again as I sit in the passenger seat while my fifteen-year-old son drives me around town. I think the brake pads on the passenger side need replacing! Yet I know that giving up control of my vehicle to my son will result in his becoming a safe driver because he has learned under my wing. I can press my imaginary brakes as much as I want, but they will neither slow nor stop the car. (Believe me, I've tried!) But if I sat and held the steering wheel and kept my foot on the real brake, my control would hinder the very thing my son needs to learn.

The greatest blessing we could ever receive is God himself.

Just like my son can't become a good driver while his mom controls the car, we can't become more Christ-like without surrendering our control to Him. The act of surrendering comes arriving at the end of ourselves allowing for the beginning of God's work in our life. When we begin to shift our focus off what we want, we start to see God working all things to His glory for those that love Him, according to His purposes (Romans 8:28). We must surrender our pride, our rights, our wants, and our needs in order to receive His blessings. The greatest blessing we could ever receive is Him.

As we go through this week, pray that God will reveal to you any area where you are trying to maintain control in your life or in the lives of others around you. Pray that God will give you the courage to surrender everything to Him.

Before you start this week, write down the top five areas of control in your life that immediately come to mind.

1. _____
2. _____
3. _____
4. _____
5. _____

Now pray God will also reveal to you those areas you try to control which you aren't aware of.

Day 1: David and Bathsheba's Choice Not to Surrender

Scripture: 2 Samuel 11

But the thing David had done displeased the Lord.
2 SAMUEL 11:27

David was a king. He was in control, and people did what he said, when he said to do it. David's title and authority should have positioned him to be even more surrendered to God. David's need for control quickly blurred the vision and the focus of his priorities, just like it can for us. David is often referred to as a man after God's own heart, and he truly loved God. However, there were many times when David decided to take control of his life instead of keeping it surrendered to God. David made several choices that severely affected his life and the lives of those around him. In 2 Samuel 11, we see David being captivated by a woman's beauty.

1. What was David's first wrong choice in 2 Samuel 11?

_____

_____

_____

David's choice to control the situation led him down a path of adultery and lies. Eventually, it led to the murder of a man who had been a friend.

2. What were the consequences that followed David's choice to control?

_____

_____

_____

David saw one way to fix the situation and instead of asking God for help, he tried to control it himself, clinging to his desires.

3. In what ways can you relate to David's desire to control a situation in order to avoid certain outcomes?

_____

_____

_____

> Billy Graham tells the story about a little child that was playing with a very valuable vase. He put his hand into it and could not withdraw it. His father too, tried his best to get it out, to no avail. They were thinking of breaking the vase when the father said, "Now my son, make one more try. Open your hand and hold your fingers out straight as you see me doing, and then pull." To [his] astonishment, the little fellow said, "Oh no, dad, I couldn't put my fingers out like that because if I did, I would drop my dime." [2]

We sometimes hold so tightly to our desires we miss the lesson of how we got there in the first place. If David had surrendered his desires—as well as his actions—to God, his friend's life would have been saved. David knew he had made a wrong choice, and the consequences that followed were life altering.

Control is the number one destroyer of relationships with family, friends, coworkers, and acquaintances. Someone is always seeking to get or maintain control.

4. Why do we so desperately seek control?

_____

_____

_____

5. In what areas of life are you most fearful of losing control?

_____

_____

_____

Our need for control can lead to bad choices with devastating consequences.

6. *If David was a man who loved God—and he was—how did he get back on track after making these terrible choices?*

_____

_____

_____

7. *How can you get back on track with your choices?*

_____

_____

_____

Day 2: Sarah's Choice Not to Surrender

Scripture: Genesis 16

You are the God who sees me,...I have now
seen the One who sees me.
GENESIS 16:13

Today's encounter is with Sarai and Abram—a couple you might know better as Sarah and Abraham. God changed their names when He changed their lives.

Sarai was a woman of God. She was full of faith and respect for God and her husband, Abram. Sarai also trusted Abram to obey God. But Sarai was barren, not able to conceive a child. In her culture, a woman's identity and value were wrapped up in her ability to give her husband a son. Sarai loved her husband and desperately wanted a child.

As the story progresses, God speaks to Abram and tells him that He will bless him with many descendants. But Abram is eighty-six years old, Sarai is seventy-six, and they do not have any children. Sarai decided that she would have to take control of the situation and find a way for Abram to have a son. Sarai then asks Abram to sleep with her maidservant, Hagar, so that he could have a child. Abram does.

1. Read Genesis 16:1–2. What thoughts do you think Sarai may have had that caused her to ask Abram to sleep with Hagar?

_____

_____

_____

Things go downhill fast between Sarai and Hagar after that. Hagar becomes pregnant, and Sarai becomes jealous.

2. Read Genesis 16:4–5. How did the feelings change between Sarai and her faithful servant, Hagar?

_____

_____

_____

Abram told Sarai to do with Hagar as she wished and so Sarai sent Hagar and her unborn baby away. Sarai's desire to control things—to make things happen—caused a firestorm around her. Her actions caused a lot of pain and a lot of hurt for everyone.

3. What are your thoughts about Sarai as she tries to handle the issue of giving Abram a son?

_____

_____

_____

In Genesis 17:1, the Lord appears again to Abram, who is now ninety-nine years old. In the course of their conversation, the Lord changes Abram's name to Abraham and Sarai's name to Sarah. The Lord often does this when He is intervening and establishing a new beginning. Think of it like a marriage when a woman takes on her new husband's name. It's a new beginning as a new person and a new relationship.

4. Read Genesis 17:17. Write down what Abraham's response was to the Lord.

_____

_____

_____

5. Read Genesis 18:10–15. How did Sarah respond to hearing the pronouncement that she would soon be pregnant? Why do you think she laughed?

_____

_____

_____

Sarah learned a hard and valuable lesson on waiting for God's timing and His blessing. Sarah learned that choosing to surrender her desires and needs to God would make way for God to bless her obedience. God had always intended to give Sarah a son. Sarah's fear of it not happening and her fear of inadequacy propelled her to take control—and it brought a lot of needless pain into their lives.

Think of a time when you decided to "make things happen" in your life because you felt this was the only way to make it happen. Have you ever made a purchase you should have waited on, forced an answer when silence was the best, or found a way around an answer that should have remained no? What happened because of your choice?

6. *Think of a time when you waited patiently for God's answer. Write down how His timing was ultimately revealed?*

_____

_____

_____

7. *Is there a time when you waited and felt you did not receive an answer? How did you handle that?*

_____

_____

_____

8. *What questions come to your mind about surrendering control?*

_____

_____

_____

Day 3: Mary's Choice to Surrender

Scripture: Luke 1:26–38; Luke 2:51

I am the Lord's servant.... May your word
to me be fulfilled.
LUKE 1:38

Mary was a thirteen-year-old girl from a Jewish family living in Nazareth, when she became engaged to a man named Joseph. The word *engaged* in that day held a deeper meaning than it does today. Today, if a couple gets engaged, they may break the engagement before the wedding without incurring any legal issues. The culture of Mary's day was a bit different. If a couple was engaged, they would have entered into a binding agreement; breaking this agreement was more like a divorce in our day.

So here we have a young teenage girl who's engaged. An angel appears to her and tells her she is going to have a baby who will be the Son of God. So many issues arise with this pronouncement! First, this young girl is engaged. Joseph can now divorce her for being pregnant with a child that is not his. More importantly, is the law which declares she could be stoned to death. There's a lot of fear surrounding this scene; however, Mary's future husband, Joseph, was a godly man who listened to the words of God. An angel visits Joseph, and Joseph chooses to follow the angel's instructions and not divorce Mary.

As a new mother-to-be in this situation, it would be difficult for Mary to surrender her fears and plans to God, especially when it concerned her life and her son. She was going to carry and raise a baby that belonged to God, knowing He was only being given to her for a season. The Bible tells us that Mary pondered these things in her heart. I imagine she had some very lonely days allowing her the time to reflect and choose where to channel her greatest fears.

1. Look at Luke 2:51 and John 2:18–19. Describe Mary as you see her.

_____

_____

_____

2. Make a list of fears that you think Mary might have felt at this point in her life.

_____

_____

_____

In an article in Christianity Today[3], Mary Fairchild points out how Mary might have felt.

> Mary must have known that her submission to God's plan would cost her. If nothing else, she knew she would be disgraced as an unwed mother. She must have thought that Joseph would divorce her, or worse yet, he might even have her put to death by stoning. Mary may not have considered the full extent of her future suffering. She may not have imagined the pain of watching her beloved child bear the weight of sin and die a terrible death on the cross. Still, she willingly submitted to God's plan. Can we willingly accept God's plan? Can we even rejoice in God's plan, like Mary did, when we know that it will cost us dearly?

God can use our pain as a means to reach others.

As I was pondering what Mary might have gone through, I realized that Mary was probably around forty-six years old when Jesus was crucified. That realization put things in a different perspective for me, since I am not far from that age myself. I began to see things from a mother's view as I looked at my own children, and my heart began to weep. Mary was well versed in the Old Testament scriptures; however, I wonder if even she understood what must eventually happen to her baby boy. The disciples were with Him for three years, and Jesus tried to tell them several times and in different ways. Even up to the last night when He ate dinner with them; they still didn't understand. Mary's faith allowed her to trust and believe from the beginning—step-by-step; day-by-day.

Just like with Mary, sometimes God chooses to use our pain as a means to reach others. Mary's pain was real and deep but also temporary. On the third day after Jesus was crucified, her belief and trust were realized. It is because of our trust and belief that our pain will be temporary. The "third day" will come again for those who believe in Jesus…for eternity!

3. *Now think about those fears listed above and make a list of the ways Mary chose to surrender them.*

_____

_____

_____

We all have wants and desires. They can rule our thoughts and drive our actions, good and bad. It's our choice to surrender to those thoughts allowing God to work His best in us. Philippians 4:6–8 tells us to surrender our negative or wrong thoughts and intentionally replace them with the things of God.

4. *Make a list of ways in which you relate to Mary. Then write out how you will choose to surrender any worries about them like Mary did.*

_____

_____

_____

Day 4: Jesus's Choice to Surrender to God

Scripture: Matthew 4:1–11; Matthew 26:36–46

My Father, if it is possible, may this cup
be taken away from Me.
Yet not as I will, but as You will.
MATTHEW 26:39

There are two times that stick out to me where Jesus had to choose to surrender His earthly desires. Read Matthew 4:1–11. The first instance was in the wilderness for forty days without water or food. Satan brought every temptation he could think of to fill those needs with earthly things. But Jesus chose to surrender His earthly desires and to lean on God for His strength. According to Strong's Dictionary, the greek word for temptation is *peirasmos*, and it means "sent by God and serving to test or prove one's character, faith, and holiness"[4]. Jesus' character was proven in the wilderness when He overcame these trials and temptations by choosing to lean on God's strength.

1. In what areas did Satan try to tempt Jesus?

_____

_____

_____

2. Why do you think Satan chose those particular areas?

_____

_____

_____

3. What classifies those areas as temptation?

_____

_____

_____

4. How did Jesus overcome those temptations?

_____

_____

_____

The second instance that we will look at is when Jesus surrendered himself to God's will in the garden of Gethsemane. Read Matthew 26: 36–46. Marks of Maturity Men's Ministry describes surrender like this:

> To surrender means to relinquish possession or control to another, to submit to the power, authority, and control of another. The entire New Testament, as summarized in Philippians 2:6–8, shows us that Christ was willing to surrender His rights and prerogatives as the second person of the Trinity to the will and purpose and plan of the Father. Then, out of that surrender came the willingness to sacrifice for God's plan no matter what the plan called for. Surrender, then, is part of the pathway to maturity and effective Christ-like ministry.[5]

Strong's Dictionary tells us the Greek word for surrender is *paradidomi*, and it means "to give into the hands of another, to give into the one's power or use" [6] This is exactly what Jesus did when He prayed in the garden the night before He was arrested to be crucified. Jesus knew what was coming, and He knew the depth of pain that He would experience physically, emotionally, and spiritually. Jesus was willing to go through pain—but *being willing* and *wanting* to do something are two different things. Jesus knew His purpose on earth, yet He asked God if there was another way. The depth of His emotions in this story shows us Jesus feels the same emotions we feel.

5. In what ways did Jesus have to choose to surrender his emotions to God?

_____

_____

_____

Jesus desperately needed time with His Father. The end was coming for Him on this earth. He was about to experience ultimate betrayal and rejection from man. All of the world's sin was about to be placed on His shoulders. He pleaded with God, "My Father, if it is possible, may this cup be taken from me. Yet not as I will, but as you will" (Matthew 26:39). The Bible also tells us that Jesus was filled with sorrow at this time.

6. *Make a list of the emotions that you think Jesus was feeling during this time.*

_____

_____

_____

God's presence is closest to us when He tells us no in the midst of our pain

Have you ever felt this way? Have you ever been in a situation where you knew God was going to do big things out of the pain you were experiencing, but you still pleaded, "God, please take this away from me"? God chose not to take it from Jesus, and sometimes He chooses not to take it from us. God's presence was never closer than that night with Jesus. God's presence is also the closest to us when He tells us "no" in the midst of our pain. Jesus sent everyone away so that He could be alone with His Father. Sometimes we also need to send everyone away so that we can hear from our Father.

7. *Is there something in your life about which God is telling you no? What choices do you have to make in order to surrender to Him through the circumstances?*

_____

_____

_____

8. *Name a time when you felt God's presence as Jesus did that night in the garden. What were the circumstances surrounding that experience?*

_____

_____

_____

Day 5: What Does Surrender Mean for Me?

Surrender yourself to the Lord and
wait patiently for Him.
PSALMS 37:7 NIV

This week we have looked at David, Sarah, Mary, and Jesus. We have seen areas where each one had to choose to surrender control in order to give their situation to God. Each person had a different struggle to deal with, that came with a choice. The choice to give in to the temptation or to surrender it to God brought forth very different outcomes for each of these people.

Left to our own strength, we would give in to temptation every time. The choice to surrender to God, however, will empower us to rely on God's strength.

1. What is God asking you to surrender?

_____

_____

_____

2. Is it hard for you to surrender to God or to a particular person? Why?

_____

_____

_____

3. What lesson could you learn through your choice to surrender control?

_____

_____

_____

4. *What are the joys that might come because of that choice? What might be the struggles?*

_____

_____

_____

5. *Consider who you are willing to answer to in your thoughts and actions. List the person or persons you allow to have authority in your life.*

_____

_____

_____

6. *In what ways are you still trying to control things in your life?*

_____

_____

_____

7. *How would those things look different if you chose to surrender them to God?*

_____

_____

_____

Lord, please forgive us for thinking we know better than You and for wanting full authority in our lives. Help us to give You the areas we try to control and help us to see the areas holding us in bondage of fear. Give us the courage and the strength to rely on Your wisdom, sovereignty, and love.

The Choice to Sacrifice

Group Discussion Questions

Be prepared to answer these questions with your group next week.

1. *Which person in the Bible did you relate to the most this week?*

    _____

    _____

    _____

    _____

    _____

    _____

2. *Is there another person in the Bible who made this same choice? Who?*

    _____

    _____

    _____

    _____

    _____

    _____

3. *How do their circumstances relate to yours?*

    _____

    _____

    _____

    _____

    _____

    _____

4. *What changes will you make in your life by choosing to love?*

    _____

    _____

    _____

    _____

    _____

    _____

WEEK 5: THE CHOICE TO SACRIFICE

Review John 15:13 to see what God has to say about sacrifice.

Day 1
1. What was God asking of Abraham?
2. Why was Abraham willing to sacrifice everything including his son?
3. What was the purpose of God's test?
4. What has God tested you with?

Day 2
1. What do you think the widow was feeling as she gave all she had?
2. What is God teaching in this story about giving?
3. Who can you relate to most, the widow or the rich people?

Day 3
1. What things did Mary sacrifice to be the mother of the Son of God?
2. In what areas did Mary have to surrender in order to sacrifice what she did?
3. What did God give to Mary because of her sacrifice?

Day 4
1. Before Jesus was even born, what did He have to sacrifice?
2. What comforts did Jesus have to sacrifice because of who He was and His ministry?
3. What sacrifice did He have to make in His relationships?
4. What was His ultimate sacrifice?

Day 5
1. What person did you relate most to this week?
2. In what areas are you sacrificing in your life?
3. What strength can you gain from others' choice to sacrifice?
4. What priority do you place on things, and is your sacrifice, a true sacrifice?

The Choice to Sacrifice

Scripture for the Week

*Greater love has no one than this, that someone lay
down his life for his friends.*
JOHN 15:13 ESV

I approached the beautiful entrance of the Fort Benning army
base one night. The grand entrance lit up with bright lights that
demanded a high level of respect. The entrance covered the four
lane highway like a bridge with a row of American flags blowing
in the wind and high columns on all four corners which proudly
boast of soldiers. It is a sight to behold. I was visiting a friend
who lived on base and I had driven this many times before, but
that night was different. As I drove under the bridge, I got chills
throughout my body as I felt a deep gratitude and appreciation for
our military. I was so thankful for the sacrifice each family makes
on a daily basis; their commitment to be married to a soldier, to
live a transient lifestyle, to raise their children in the absence of
a spouse, and to put their own lives in danger. Every military
family faces a reality of risk on a level that most nonmilitary
people never face. These thoughts consumed my heart and mind
as I drove on to the base.

After you pass the grand entrance everyone is required to stop at a
security gate where an officer verifies your ID. The officer handed
my ID back and said, "Welcome home." This was a phrase that
they said to everyone as they entered the base. Whether you
actually lived on base or were a part of the military didn't matter
at that moment, you were part of the reason they existed; part of
a mission to protect our freedom. *"Welcome Home"* *Wow.* What a

sense of community and belonging—I could feel it, even though I was not in the military. I arrived at my friend's home nestled among a cluster of colonial homes where soldiers of all ranks lived with their families. This is a huge community who supports one another and loves each other as family. This community knows all to well the meaning of living for someone and something greater than ourselves. We later left base for dinner and upon returning that evening, an officer again took our ID and said "Take it easy, and welcome home."

What would life be like if we chose to "take it easy", and to say to others, "welcome home"? I'm in no way suggesting being a Christian is easy, but I am saying having a relationship that you can lean on to get you through trials and struggles is much easier than attempting to do everything in your own strength. Jesus tells us His yoke is lighter than ours, and we can trade ours for His. Jesus is telling us to "take it easy". As a Christian, we are part of a community of believers. We should be there to welcome each other home when we fail and encourage each other to take it easy when we need rest.

When God asks us to sacrifice, it is always for our gain, though sometimes it is in a realm we just can't see.

The military understands this, but I am not so sure all Christians do. The military understands the cost of sacrifice, but do we? What are we willing to give up on a daily basis? Sometimes we aren't even willing to give up time to wait in a drive-thru, much less to sacrifice any desires for a righteous cause. Sacrifice is something we must understand and be willing to do. It's what Jesus did so that we might live. Our eternity rests on our understanding of who Jesus is and the sacrifice that He made for us.

Why would God ask us to sacrifice if Jesus has already done it? God wants everything that is hindering our relationship with Him removed. If giving up something is a sacrifice for us, then we can lean on God to get us through. Giving something up is only a sacrifice if it costs us something. Sacrifice cost God everything, including His only Son. Why do we feel so unjustly treated when we are asked to sacrifice? Why do we value things and people above our relationship with God?

Over the next five days, we are going to look at people who were called to sacrifice. They each had to choose to give up something they held close, and their choice would cost them dearly, but they each stood to gain so much more because of their choice. They each would gain a deeper trust and faith in God, along with His provision, love, and guidance. When God asks us to sacrifice, it is always for our gain; though sometimes it's in a realm that we just can't see. When we begin to see God in the sacrifice, we can take it easy and rest in Him, and then He says back to us, "Welcome Home!"

Day 1: Abraham's Choice to Sacrifice

Scripture: Genesis 22

God Himself will provide.
GENESIS 22:8

Abraham was promised by God to give him a son, however it wasn't until Abraham was one hundred years old that God fulfilled His promise by giving him Isaac. Abraham had a long history of waiting on God and trusting His Word to be true, so when asked by God to take his only son and sacrifice him on an altar, he obeyed without question. This request must have seemed crazy to Abraham but the Bible tells us Abraham's response was simply, "Here I am" (vs. 1, 11). This was the ultimate sacrifice. The very legacy Abraham was promised to carry on his name was now being asked to become a sacrifice. God intervened in the last moment and told Abraham to stop. God provided a ram in the thicket beside Abraham that was used as a sacrifice, a replacement for Abraham's only son. (v.13-14). This was the same act God would carry out to completion many years later with His own Son. The sacrifice was more about Abraham and God than about Abraham and his son. This was a huge test by God to see if Abraham was trustworthy enough to sacrifice everything that might be put before God. Abraham called the mountain, Mt. Moriah, "The Lord Will Provide" because God not only intervened and saved his son's life but God also blessed him and "made his descendants as numerous as the stars in the sky and as the sand on the seashore"(v.17) because of his willingness to obey and sacrifice everything for God. God's command signified how far He himself was willing to go for us, with out requiring us to go that far for Him.

1. Why do you think God tested Abraham?

_____

_____

_____

God had big plans to use Abraham and his faith in mighty ways, but He had to know if he was trustworthy in his obedience, trust, and faith in God. God would provide the ultimate sacrifice, and He needed to know if Abraham was willing to do the same. Would Abraham put God first? Was he willing to sacrifice and give up everything God asked?

2. What did God ask Abraham to do first?

_____

_____

_____

3. What was Abraham's first response to God?

_____

_____

_____

I have always had the utmost respect for foreign missionaries. When I was young, my church supported a missionary, Martha Wade through Pioneer Bible Translators. One year, my father went with a group of men to help build her a home in Papua New Guinea. It took a month of traveling through the jungle to get to the town where Martha lived. Martha was there to translate the Bible into the native language, so the people living in the jungle could hear the Word of God. Martha needed a home to protect her and she needed nets around her home that would keep out mosquitos known for infecting people with malaria. The group of men from our church went days traveling by plane, foot, and boat to provide the necessities for her. The living conditions by our standards were awful. I was always amazed by Martha's choice to sacrifice the comforts of life here in America to life in the jungle.

God calls each of us to the place He can use us in the greatest way.

I remember verbally saying, "God, I want to be a good Christian, but just not THAT good of one." I thought that God called the "best Christians" to go overseas, to places like Africa and New Guinea. I wanted to be good enough to be used, as long as I didn't have to sacrifice my comforts. I have since realized that God calls us all, and the place to which we are called is not an indication of how good we are. God calls each of us to the place He can use us in the greatest way. The "good Christians," as we might label them, are people who choose to sacrifice their desires of temporary satisfaction for eternal satisfaction in the things of God. God called Abraham to obey in the moment, to make a sacrifice beyond anything he could possibly imagine on this earth. Abraham's sacrifice called for obedience with each step and each decision, all while listening to God's voice guide him.

4. What was the result of Abraham's willingness to sacrifice?

_____

_____

_____

What if Abraham had been so upset or worried about what God had called him to do that he missed hearing God's direction to change course, and thus, the huge blessing of growing his relationship with God?

5. How do you feel about the way God tested Abraham?

_____

_____

_____

God's questions have not changed. He wants to know if we are willing to go with Him and to let go of every tear, pain, desire, relationship, and feeling, trusting Him with the outcome.

6. Has there been a time in your life where you felt God was testing you or asking you to sacrifice something? What was it?

_____

_____

_____

7. What was your initial response?

_____

_____

_____

8. What was the result of your choice?

_____

_____

_____

9. What is God calling you to sacrifice today?

_____

_____

_____

Day 2: The Widow's Choice to Sacrifice

Scripture: Luke 21:1–4

She, out of her poverty, put in all
that she had to live on.
LUKE 21:4

In order to truly recognize what sacrifice is, we must know the difference between choosing to surrender and choosing to sacrifice. Surrendering requires a struggle. The term implies that there are two wills at conflict, and one must submit to the other in order to move forward. Sacrifice, on the other hand, is a willing heart who gives up something that one needs, values, or treasures for something that is greater than oneself. Surrender and sacrifice are both choices, but sacrifice is not about saying, "Okay, you win; I'll do it your way." Sacrifice is a choice to give up something you treasure or value for a greater purpose. Sacrifice is about choosing to go without something in this world in order to realize that only God can satisfy your deepest needs.

Often our sacrifice can go unrecognized or seem insignificant to everyone but God. But our sacrifice will never go unnoticed by the One for whom we are sacrificing.

> **Our sacrifice will never go unnoticed by the One for whom we are sacrificing**

Fill in the blanks: Luke 21:1–2 says that Jesus _____ the rich. He also _____ a poor widow. In verse 3, Jesus tells His disciples that _____ has put in more than all the others.

1. Why do you think Jesus says this?

_____
_____
_____

In this passage, Jesus tells us about a widowed woman who chose to give all she had to God. Doing so left her penniless—she would have to trust God to provide food for her children. She took her only two coins to the temple for the yearly offering. She had to walk beside people who had everything to offer in contrast to her. The rich gave a portion of their wealth, and they took pride in what they gave. But their offerings didn't cost them anything.

Fill in the blanks: *In verse 4, Jesus says that the rich gave out of their _____ but the widow gave out of her _____.*

This story doesn't tell us the woman's name; it only tells us that she was a poor widow. The widow's level of sacrifice seemed to fall short of all the people she had to walk past who gave far more monetarily. But the level of sacrifice chosen by this widow was far greater, because it involved her heart and her trust in God. It was an example of what true sacrifice looks like.

Sacrifice is true selflessness. As we mentioned in the intro to this week, our soldiers and their families live a sacrificial life. They put their lives on the line every day because they make a choice to give of themselves for the greater good of our nation.

2. *Can you recall a time in your life when you gave sacrificially to God or to another person?*

_____
_____
_____

3. *Write out the details of what happened because of your choice to sacrifice.*

_____
_____
_____

A true choice of sacrifice is not a delay of gratification. It is a decision that redefines who and what we receive satisfaction from. There are many times I have delayed getting what I wanted, but I knew I would eventually be able to have what I wanted, so my giving wasn't truly sacrificial. Sacrifice should always end with God. He knows the ultimate sacrifice, and He knows what

He calls us to give up so that He can bless us with a deeper relationship with Him.

4. *Can you identify an area where you previously had to make a choice to sacrifice?*

_____

_____

_____

Pray that God reveals an area in your life where you need to choose to sacrifice. For example, it could be finances, relationships, time, or health. Pray that your eyes will be opened to see what area could be hindering a closer walk with God.

5. *Write down what comes to mind first and then spend time in prayer over it.*

_____

_____

_____

Remember, Jesus didn't give us the widow's name. It's never the person but the heart of the action that is important. Give others the same respect and keep the focus on their actions and heart, not the name of the person.

6. *How do you think the widow felt waiting in line to give her offering?*

_____

_____

_____

7. *Have you ever been in a similar situation where you felt the amount you had to give was inadequate or insufficient compared to those around you?*

_____

_____

_____

8. *Which do you most relate to — the rich people or the widow?*

_____

_____

_____

Day 3: Mary's Choice to Sacrifice

Scripture: Luke 2:1–21

While they were {in Bethlehem}, the time came for the baby to be born, and she gave birth to her firstborn, a son. She wrapped him in cloths and placed him in a manger, because there was no guest room available for them.
Luke 2:6–7 (NIV)

Mary was the mother of Jesus, the Son of God. She was given that honor because God found her trustworthy and faithful. She wasn't perfect, however—she struggled with the same decisions and was faced with choices just like we are today. What made Mary such an incredible role model and powerful influence in our lives was that she made the right choice in the eyes of God. She chose to submit, love, obey, trust, surrender, and sacrifice. The road that Mary was asked to walk was one of faith. She was given much, and she would have to sacrifice much. God called her to a life that would endure great pain, but He also gave her Jesus to get her through it.

Being a Christian, a follower of Christ is also a walk of faith. It requires us to sacrifice our earthly desires so we might gain Jesus himself. *Webster's Dictionary* defines sacrifice as "to give up (something that you want to keep) especially in order to get or do something else or to help someone." [7] Mary made the choice to sacrifice.

Mary's life seemed to be a normal one for a young girl from Nazareth. When Mary was only thirteen, she became engaged to a young carpenter named Joseph. Sometime during their engagement, an angel appeared to Mary and told her she was going to be with child and that she would give birth to the Son of God. This presented some huge issues for Mary. The baby was not Joseph's—this meant he could either divorce her or have her stoned to death. The angel had appeared to Mary but not to Joseph, and Joseph had to be convinced that she had not betrayed him. I have often thought that God could have made this so much easier if the angel had appeared to them together, *right?* But God sent an angel to Joseph in a dream and told him to stay with Mary. Mary and Joseph both had choices to make, and they chose to walk this hard and painful road with God. Mary's role as the mother of Jesus did not keep her from the same struggles that we encounter. She had to teach Jesus to become a man, to eat with His mouth closed, to stop running in the house. She would lose sleep and be exhausted. She would have to tell her child to stop, she had to say no a thousand times. On the other hand, she gained a sidekick to enjoy and to love with all her heart.

Being a Christian requires us to sacrifice our earthly desires so we might gain Jesus himself

Fill in the blanks: In Luke 2:52, we read that "Jesus grew in _____ and _____ and in favor with God and man."

1. Write out Isaiah 7:14–15.

_____

_____

_____

Jesus would learn what was right and what was wrong, and Jesus would have to choose to do right! If Jesus had the choice, you bet we do, too. We get to choose the right instead of the wrong. Mary chose the right. Mary chose to sacrifice the plans and dreams she had as a girl to do what God was asking of her at this time in her life.

2. Do you feel that Mary faced the same fears as we might today?

_____

_____

_____

3. What fears as a child would Mary be forced to face?

_____

_____

_____

4. What fears as a mother would Mary have to face?

_____

_____

_____

5. What things would Mary have to give up or let go of because of this new role?

_____

_____

_____

6. Has God ever asked you to set aside your plans to fulfill His will for your life?

_____

_____

_____

We all have to choose to sacrifice something every day. Sometimes it's a big sacrifice, like sending our loved ones to the mission field; sometimes it's giving up our life dream to help someone else succeed at theirs, and sometimes it's the daily choice of giving up our desires for the greater good of someone else. Sacrifice can come in many forms—sometimes in our jobs, homes, children, spouses, or desires. Sacrifice is laying down our rights for something better, for God's purposes.

7. Name some areas in which you feel you have sacrificed.

_____

_____

_____

Mary did not get recognition or praise for her sacrifice. Most of what Mary had to sacrifice in her life was private and went unrecognized by everyone. Most of what we know about Mary is that she "treasured up all these things and pondered them in her heart" (Luke 2:19 and Luke 2:51).

8. *In what ways is the choice to sacrifice the hardest decision in your life?*

_____

_____

_____

9. *Is it harder to sacrifice when no one realizes or recognizes that you are doing so?*

_____

_____

_____

10. *If an angel appeared to you today, what area of your life would he ask you to sacrifice for God?*

_____

_____

_____

11. *In which life stage do you think sacrifice is the most prevalent for us today?*

_____

_____

_____

Day 4: Jesus's Choice to Sacrifice

Scripture: Luke 19:1–10

For the Son of Man came to seek and to save the lost.
LUKE 19:10

A Sacrifice must cost us something that is important.

Jesus chose a life that was almost nomadic. He never owned a home because He was constantly on the move to meet and influence new people. For example, Luke 19:1–10 tells us the story of Jesus going to a tax collector's home. Luke 10:38–42 tells us about His visits with Mary and Martha. Luke 4:38 tells us Jesus stayed at the home of Simon. Jesus's ministry on earth meant sacrificing the material comforts of this world. I wonder if at times, His feet became sore or if He was hungry or tired? Living a life as a guest in other people's homes can be exhausting. Have you ever been on a trip for an extended period, like a mission trip, camp, or a nice vacation? No matter how nice or difficult the location, we all look forward to returning to the comforts of our home. We look forward to our own shower and our own bed. The fact that Jesus never had a home on earth is a lesson to us that while He was here, this was not His home. The comforts of His home were in Heaven. Just like we long to be in our home, He longed to be back in heaven. Maybe Jesus was trying to tell us that this is not our home either. Maybe He needed us to see that our homes and our things are temporary, and we need to treat them as such. Our home is yet to come.

Jesus sacrificed a lot in material things, but sacrificing is only a sacrifice if it cost something that is important to you. I would venture to say; those things were not important to Jesus. The significant sacrifice Jesus made was to leave His rightful throne, next to God, to come to us.

1. *Read Philippians 2:5–8. In your own words, summarize what you think these verses mean.*

_____

_____

_____

Before Jesus took His first breath on this earth, His choice to sacrifice for us began in heaven. He would have to humble Himself to His creation and teach us to serve by serving us. He would have to leave His rightful throne, the continual presence of God, and the perpetual glory of heaven itself. (John 1:1, Genesis 1:26, John 1:15, and John 6:38–40 all refer to the fact that Jesus existed with God in the beginning). Because we have yet to experience heaven, we can't truly understand the sacrifice that Jesus made to come to earth.

2. *Has there ever been a time when you made a huge sacrifice for your children, but they never knew or could not comprehend the sacrifice at the time?*

_____

_____

_____

That's what Jesus did for us. He sacrificed greatly before we would ever know or comprehend the depth of His love for us.

The other sacrifice He made was to give up His life on earth so that we might live in heaven eternally with Him. Have you ever seen the movies, *Passion of Christ*, the *Bible Story,* or most recently the *Son of God?* If you have seen one of them, think back to the physical pain that Jesus endured. These movies intentionally try to bring our focus and realization to the depths Jesus physically suffered. He felt every lash that beat His back, every drop of blood that stung the cuts and sores all over Him. He felt every hit of the hammer as the nails pierced His hands and feet. He felt every thorn which pierced His head. He sacrificed so much. Jesus

Jesus chose right instead of wrong and the best instead of the better to accomplish the will of God

chose to become the sacrifice for the greater good. He chose right instead of wrong and the best instead of the better to accomplish the will of God.

3. *What things do you think Jesus gave up that we might feel are everyday comforts or even our rights?*

_____

_____

_____

4. *Do you see Jesus's life on this earth as a mission or a sacrifice? Why?*

_____

_____

_____

5. *How do you think Jesus felt as He looked down from the cross and saw His mother, Mary? Refer to John 19:26–27.*

_____

_____

_____

6. *Considering the magnitude of Jesus' sacrifice, how do you think He feels when we resist the call to sacrifice?*

_____

_____

_____

7. *How can you change your definition of sacrifice in your personal life to align with what our Lord and Savior truly sacrificed for us?*

_____

_____

_____

Day 5: What Does Sacrifice Mean for Me?

*I appeal to you therefore, brothers, by the mercies
of God, to present your bodies as a living sacrifice,
holy and acceptable to God, which is your spiritual
worship. Do not be conformed to this world, but be
transformed by the renewal of your mind, that by
testing you may discern what is the will of God, what
is good and acceptable and perfect*
ROMANS 12:1-2 ESV

Sacrifice is hard to grasp for us living in America. We are a nation of entitlement and we rarely have to sacrifice for our wants, even more rarely for our needs. We have become very good at making things happen when we want and doing only the things that we want to do. Sacrifice for us may look more like doing what others need instead of only what we want, when we want. We get to choose where we go to church, what ministry we like the most, and who we get to help. But maybe—just maybe—God is calling us to listen and to serve beyond our comfort level so that we may encounter yet another side of our loving Father. That is sacrifice.

1. In what areas do you need to make a choice to sacrifice your own needs and desires?

_____

_____

_____

2. Do you struggle with sacrifice?

_____

_____

_____

3. *Does sacrifice always have to be hard or painful? Why or why not?*

_____

_____

_____

4. *What is your own definition of sacrifice? What does it look like in other people around you?*

_____

_____

_____

Lord, teach us to live for You. Teach us to want what You desire for our lives so that we may lay down all the worldly influences for You. Lord, change our vision and our thoughts to seek You and You alone so that we are willing to forfeit, or sacrifice anything to gain You.

The Choice to Trust

Be prepared to answer these questions with your group next week.

1. *Which person in the Bible did you relate to the most this week?*

_____

_____

_____

_____

_____

_____

2. *Is there another person in the Bible who made this same choice? Who?*

_____

_____

_____

_____

_____

_____

3. *How do their circumstances relate to yours?*

_____

_____

_____

_____

_____

_____

4. *What changes will you make in your life by choosing to love?*

_____

_____

_____

_____

_____

_____

WEEK 6: TRUST

Leader's Questions for Week Six: The Choice to Trust

Review Proverbs 3:5–6 to see what God says about trusting Him.

Day 1

1. In what area of her life was she forced to trust someone?
2. What was the most difficult choice Ruth had to make?
3. In what ways did Ruth fully trust God in spite of her fears?

Day 2

1. Who did Esther choose to trust in her life?
2. What did Esther have to gain by trusting God and what did she have to lose by not?
3. What lives were changed because of Esther's choices?

Day 3

1. What were Shadrach, Meshach, and Abednego willing to give up because of their trust in God?
2. How did their level of trust increase with their level of obedience?
3. What risks did they take to trust in God?
4. What benefits and blessings did they receive because of their trust in God?

Day 4

1. Who did Jesus entrust with his mission on this earth and why did he choose each one?
2. What was Jesus's response when His trust was betrayed?
3. How do you respond when your trust is betrayed?

Day 5

1. What person did you relate most to this week?
2. In what areas of your life do you struggle with trust?
3. What does trusting require of you?
4. How does trust affect and reflect your relationship with God?

The Choice to Trust

Scripture for the Week

Trust in the Lord with all your heart, and lean not on your own understanding; in all your ways acknowledge Him, and He shall direct your path.
PROVERBS 3:5-6 NKJV

Trust. I thought I had this one in the pocket. I was so excited to finish the study with this topic because I thought it would be an easy one for me. I thought I had conquered the issue of trust many, many years ago. I was stunned when I got to this week and hit an unexpected roadblock. This was a huge boulder for me because I have always trusted God. I can look back and count the times when my life depended on my choice to trust Him. I trusted that God was sovereign and that He loved His children. I trusted that He loved me. I trusted that He could and would do what was best according to His plan. He always had, and I believed He always would. It wasn't until I sat down to write this study that God revealed to me that I hadn't chosen to trust Him with the everyday issues of my life and of those around me. I knew He had the "big" things under control, and I chose to trust Him in those. But I had never realized I didn't trust Him in the ongoing events or struggles that I live out daily.

God showed it to me this way—picture a child running to the park, parent running right beside her, ready to help and push her on the swings. The young girl gets herself up in the swings but because she doesn't know how to pump her legs, she sits. The parent walks up to give her little girl a good push, and she quickly says, "No, Mommy (or Daddy), I got this!" So the parent steps back and the girl sits frustrated and trying, but still not moving. She gets down and runs to the monkey bars. She is little, so she starts jumping up and down, each time reaching for the bar that is still five feet above her head. The parent comes over to pick her up and help her with her struggle. "Why don't you let me handle this for you, I'm a little bigger and I can lift you up," the parent suggests. The little girl replies, "No, I got this!" And she continues to jump but never even comes close to overcoming her struggle or the issue she currently faces. She finally gives up and moves on to her next interest, where she again declares, "I've got this!"

The little girl is so determined to conquer her struggles on her own she exhausts her strength without ever receiving the joy and blessing of all the park had to offer. She probably enjoyed the sand, but if she had chosen to trust her parents to guide her through her struggles, her joy would have doubled.

God is standing with me every day, ready to help me with every struggle, ready to give me a push in the right direction and to lift me up when I keep falling down. He is such a gentleman and a loving parent that He won't impose Himself on me. I have to choose to accept His offer. God wants to help me in everyday issues and in my every struggle. Our everyday struggles (to love, obey, forgive, surrender, sacrifice and trust) often make it more difficult for us to depend on God than life altering devastating tragedies, which hit us unexpectedly.

Ecclesiastes 3:1 tells us, "There is a time for everything, and a season for every activity under the heavens." There is a time to struggle, and great things are taught in our struggles, but there is also a time to rest. If the child on the playground had chosen to rest in her parent's arms, she would have soared higher on her swing and climbed higher and longer on the monkey bars on her parent's strength instead of her own. First Peter 5:7 says, "Cast all your cares upon Him, for He cares for you." God cares when we struggle. He cares about every struggle that we have, the big ones as well as the little ones.

God calls us to trust Him with the every day issues in our life and the lives of those around us

We must choose to trust God for who He is and what He will do in the midst of our struggles and pain

As we have gone through the last six weeks looking at love, obedience, forgiveness, surrender, and sacrifice, there is one thread that ties all these together. None of these choices will be made unless we choose first to trust God. We must make the choice to trust God to be who He says He is; we must trust God will do what He says He will do. We won't choose to love, obey, forgive, surrender, or sacrifice unless we deem the receiver trustworthy. God is the ultimate receiver of our choices. If we do everything for Him, then day-to-day issues and the responses of everyone around us will begin to quiet as we listen to the words of the only One who is truly trustworthy in ALL things. This is a choice we must make to trust God for who He is and what He will do in the midst of all our struggles and pain.

In the coming week, we will look at Ruth, Esther and three men who risked their lives for God. As we dive into their lives and see the choices they made to trust God in the midst of their struggles, we will discover a level of trust, which forms a foundation for every choice we make.

Day 1: Ruth's Choice to Trust

Scripture: Ruth 1–4

Don't urge me to leave you or to turn back from you.
Where you go I will go, and where you stay I will stay.
Your people will be my people and your God my God.
RUTH 1:16

I hope you read the whole book of Ruth. I love this story and this woman. She is the epitome of selflessness and love. Ruth met and married a man from a foreign land who had been raised with a different religion and culture than she had been. Despite their differences, Ruth developed a wonderful relationship with her mother-in-law. The land they lived in went through a terrible famine and took the lives of her husband, father-in-law, and brother-in-law. Ruth, Naomi, and her sister-in-law Orpah were left to figure how to move on. The Jewish culture of the day was such that a woman's purpose and value was in her ability to bear children for her husband. If the man died, then his brother was to marry the woman and have children with her, in order to carry on and honor his deceased brother's name and legacy. If the husband didn't have a brother, then his next of kin would take on that responsibility.

Once the famine was over, Naomi decided to return to her homeland. Naomi pleaded with the girls to leave her and go find husbands who could provide for them. After some convincing, Orpah did just that. Ruth, however, was determined to stay with Naomi. Their close and deep relationship enabled Naomi to introduce Ruth to her God. Ruth did not want to leave the one person who had given her hope in this world. Naomi showed Ruth the way to God, and Ruth's response to Naomi was reflective of that hope.

Write out Ruth 1:16.

_____

_____

_____

Let's look at some choices that Ruth had to make.

Ruth chose to trust that Naomi's God was real and He was worthy of her trust. Ruth was not raised in a Christian home. She didn't grow up knowing the scriptures; she learned about who God was from Naomi. Ruth and Naomi were about to experience God's faithfulness together.

1. Has someone else's personal walk enabled you or challenged you to make the choice to trust God for yourself? If so, who?

_____

_____

_____

Ruth chose to stay with Naomi and to help provide and take care of her. Ruth chose to do what was right because she trusted first. True obedience requires trust. Ruth trusted Naomi, and because of that trust she was willing to sacrifice and surrender everything to follow the one she trusted, and she was blessed for it. Read Ruth 2:2–3. Notice that Ruth's blessing came after her choice to trust.

2. Write about a time in your life when your blessing followed your choice to trust.

_____

_____

_____

Ruth chose to move to a foreign land with Naomi and become the foreigner that her husband had been in her land (verse 18). Ruth had to trust God on many levels. She had to trust Him in the big things, like moving to a foreign land that was a known enemy of her birth home. She had to trust Him daily, to provide a place to work, food on the table, acceptance, and more.

3. Identify the BIG things requiring you to trust God in your life.

_____

_____

_____

4. Identify the LITTLE things requiring you to trust God in your life.

_____

_____

_____

5. Which one is easier to trust God with?

_____

_____

_____

There were many areas where Ruth had to choose to trust. Ruth had to trust God would provide for her needs. She trusted that He would handle the details, so she listened to His voice and she chose to obey as she trusted. And God proved Himself faithful. When Boaz met Ruth, he promised her some things.

6. Write out what Boaz instructed Ruth to do (Ruth 2:8–9).

_____

_____

_____

God can take our good choices and our bad choices and use them to His glory in a way we have never experienced before

I want you to see the full picture here. Ruth left her life to live among a people she didn't know, who worshipped a God she had not known. God placed Ruth in the fields belonging to Boaz—her kinsman-redeemer, the next male relation who would legally have the right to bring her into his family and take care of her and Naomi.

God orchestrated every step, weaving together the choices that they made, to show His glory in ways they had never known before. God does this for us. He takes the good choices and the bad choices, and He uses them to His glory in a way we have never known before. We have the choice to see Him and know He is working even when we don't see Him, because we trust who He says He is and what He says He will do.

Day 2: Esther's Choice to Trust

Scripture: Esther 4
(The book of Esther is only 10 chapters, we will
focus mainly on chapter 4 but you will get a deeper
understanding if you read the entire book.)

*Who knows but that you have come into your
royal position for such a time as this?*
ESTHER 4:14

Esther's life had been hard. She had lost her mother and father at a young age and was being raised by her uncle Mordecai. He loved her as his own and raised her to trust God. During this time in history, Xerxes was king. He had dismissed his wife from her role as queen and his presence because she refused to come to him. This left a vacancy in the royal house. Chapter 2 tells us that the king's servants brought every beautiful, young, virgin girl to the palace for a year, where they went through extensive beauty treatments. The one who ultimately pleased the king would be made queen (2:3–4). Esther was included in the group of girls who were brought to the palace. Verse 10 tells us that Mordecai directed Esther not to tell anyone of her Jewish nationality or family background, and she obeyed. Esther's natural beauty was captivating. She was admired by everyone who saw her, and she won the king over (2:15). Esther became the new queen.

Mordecai kept watch over Esther from afar, and when word on the street came that the king was in danger, he sent word to Esther. Sometime later, an evil man named Haman talked the king into making a decree to kill all the Jews in their land. This would, of course, include all of Esther's family. At this time, it still had not been revealed that Queen Esther was a Jew. It was now up to Queen Esther to petition the king to stop this proclamation. In this day, no one could enter the king's presence without being summoned. If, by chance, someone did enter his presence without invitation, the king must hold out his golden scepter or the person would die. Esther's people fasted and prayed for her as she prepared to go before the king.

1. Mordecai told Esther that she had been placed in her position "_____ _____ _____ _____ _____ _____" (4:14), in order to help save her people—God's people.

Esther had to trust God that He had placed her right where He needed her, using her to His glory. She had to trust Him with her life and her family's lives. Esther chose to trust God, and He used her to save His people.

Esther's life had been filled with tragedy, but God brought her through those trials and blessed her greatly. It was through her pain that she was positioned into Mordecai's life and later positioned in the city of King Xerxes at just the appointed time. God's plan was to use her tragedy for good, and because she trusted Him, He was able to use her in a mighty way.

2. Name a time when God used your pain and made something good come from it.

_____

_____

_____

Esther's pain was used for good in her own life because she chose to trust God. Can we trust God to use our pain? Can we trust Him to make something good from our pain?

3. What if Esther hadn't chosen to trust God? How might the circumstances have ended differently?

_____

_____

_____

Mordecai tells Esther in 4:14, "If you remain silent at this time, relief and deliverance for the Jews will arise from another place,

> **Esther's life had been filled with tragedy but God brought her through the trials and blessed her greatly**

but you and your father's family will perish." Those are harsh words, but they apply to us today as well. If we choose to trust God and allow His glory to be shown in our lives, then we will receive the blessing of His deliverance in our lives. If however, we choose to not trust God, then deliverance and relief will come for someone else who did make the choice to trust.

God has placed each of us in the position we are in for *such a time as this*. We all have struggles, and we all have pain. What we do with the choice to trust will determine the outcome of our deliverance. He wants to impact us through our circumstances. He also wants to use us and our circumstances to impact others.

Day 3: Shadrach, Meshach, and Abednego's Choice to Trust

Scripture: Daniel 3

They trusted in him and defied the king's command and were willing to give up their lives rather than serve or worship any god except their own God.
DANIEL 3:28

King Nebecenezzer was an evil king who wanted people to worship only him. Three men, Shadrach, Meshach, and Abednego chose not to bow down and worship the King when commanded and were thrown into a fiery furnace because of their belief and stance on God. The King wanted to make a statement that his subjects were not to defy him, so he had the furnace turned up so high several guards died of the heat as they approached the furnace itself. The three men were thrown into this fiery furnace but what happened next changed all their lives. As everyone watched, there was suddenly four men instead of three in the fire. The people counted again, but it was true. As the men in the fire stood firm in trusting God, God showed up. He was in the fire with them. He was their strength, their refuge. I guarantee that the three men were not focused on what the others were doing outside of the fire at this point. Their focus was on God. Their power source had met them where they were. Because the men choose to trust God even before the fire came, it was easier for them to trust God when it was time to be thrown into the fire. Not only was God protecting and sustaining them inside the fire, but His glory shown outside the fire. The people who were gathered around to see the men now questioned, *who is the fourth man?* Their focus was now off the three and onto *the One*! They saw that the men were not consumed, but brought through the flames because of who was with them.

Oh, dear friends, this tragic situation—*your* tragic situation—is showing nothing else but God's glory! He will not only stand by you getting you through your heartaches; He will go into the fire with you! As you turn your focus on Him, you will cause others to question who is sustaining you. Who is the One helping you?

> **As you go through the fire, people will ask who is sustaining you.**

1. What did King Nebuchadnezzar expect the men to do? (Daniel 3:5–6).

_____

_____

_____

2. In what areas did God require trust from these men?

_____

_____

_____

3. What did these men have to give up to trust God?

_____

_____

_____

4. How did their level of trust increase with their level of obedience?

_____

_____

_____

5. What risks did they take to trust in God?

_____

_____

_____

6. What benefits and blessings did they receive from trusting God?

_____

_____

_____

Read Daniel 3:17–18 and fill in the blanks: *"If we are thrown into the blazing furnace, the God we serve ___ ____ ___ ____ _____ from it, and He will deliver us from Your Majesty's hand. _____ _____ _____ ____ ____ _____, we want you to know, Your Majesty, that we will never serve your gods or worship the image of gold you have set up."*

The three men knew without a doubt that God was able to save them. They trusted God to protect them, whether that meant *from* the fire or *in* the fire. The game changer here is the second part, "But even if He doesn't…!" These men were choosing to trust God even if He didn't save them on this side of heaven. Their love and their trust for God did not change with their circumstances; it gave them courage to trust God's Word.

Here is where our trust and faith are shaken to the core. We trust God when He responds the way we want Him too. We trust Him when we see Him work miracles, but what happens when we see Him do the opposite? What happens when we pray to be saved from our worst struggles, and instead of taking us away from them, He allows us to go right through the middle of them? What happens to our faith and our level of trust when we don't see God because of the smoke?

Isaiah 55:9 tells us that God's thoughts are not our thoughts, neither are His ways our ways. The three men based their level of trust on <u>who</u> God was, not on <u>what</u> He did or would do. The very essence of who God is never changes.

- If God was ever trustworthy, then He still is.
- If God was ever love, then He still is.
- If God ever wanted the best for us, then He still does.

If our trust, just like the three men, is based on who God is, then our trust will weather any storm or any fire. So many times we ask God why, because we don't understand His ways. The Bible says it's okay that we don't understand. Our trust is a choice that

The men trusted God to protect them, whether that meant from the fire or in the fire.

Their trust was based on <u>who</u> God was, not on <u>what</u> He did or would do.

should not waiver. If it does, our focus is probably not on who God is, but rather on the limited circumstances we are allowed to experience and see. He wants us to trust Him enough to say, even if He doesn't remove the fire, we will still choose to trust Him.

7. *Write down a time when you were thrown into the fire. Describe your choice to trust Him in the midst of it.*

_____

_____

_____

8. *At what point in your experience was the choice to trust the hardest? Was there a point when you stopped trusting and felt it was time for you to handle it?*

_____

_____

_____

9. *What blessings have you received because of your choice to trust God?*

_____

_____

_____

Day 4: Jesus's Choice to Trust

Scripture: John 19:26-27, Matthew 28:19-20,

You therefore, my son, be strong in the grace that is in Christ Jesus. The things which you have heard from me in the presence of many witnesses, entrust these to faithful men who will be able to teach others also.
2 TIMOTHY 2:1-2

This week we have looked at people who made the choice to trust. Today as we look at Jesus we will see that He is the rock who can be trusted. When we choose to trust Him, He entrusts us.

One example is in John 19:26-27 where Jesus is dying on the cross and He entrusts his mother to John. Jesus handpicked John to take care of His mother. John's love for his Savior and prior obedience prepared him to take care of Jesus' own mother.

1. *Write out John 19:26-27*

_____
_____
_____

2. *What do these verses mean to you?*

_____
_____
_____

3. *Is Jesus entrusting you with someone who is in a difficult season? What is He asking of you?*

_____
_____
_____

God entrusted us all to share the gospel with everyone

Another example is Jesus' choice to entrust His disciples to spread the Good News. In Matthew 28:16-20, Jesus tells the disciples "all authority in Heaven and on earth has been given to Me." He has the authority to entrust us with His mission, to command us to live a life that reflects the life that He lived here on earth.

4. *Write out Matthew 28:19 -20.*

_____

_____

_____

Jesus taught them what they needed to know. The message came from Jesus. He is the message. All the disciples had to do was listen and believe. Now Jesus is saying, the gospel is not just for you, but go tell others. He entrusts the disciples with the message of the gospel.

5. *Jesus entrusted His disciples to carry the Good News to all the world. How are you obeying this command?*

_____

_____

_____

Lastly, Jesus left us with His words, the Living Word. He gave us a blueprint that we are entrusted to learn and live by. The Bible details everything we need to know to establish a right relationship with our Lord and Savior. The Bible is our lifeline and our source of strength in our time of need, but it is also the very thing that opens our hearts and minds to know more of our Creator. Psalm 119:11 says, "I have hidden your word in my heart that I might not sin against you." God wants us to know Him, so He graciously wrote His story down for us to hold in our hands and hide in our hearts. As we read and believe His word, we realize the treasure we have. Christ in us. Our treasure is too great to keep to ourselves, and God's love prompts us to share it with others. He is entrusting us to do this!! Memorize, ponder, treasure and apply it to your life.

6. *Work on Memorizing Psalm 119:11! You can do this!*

7. *Write about a time in your life when the Word of God encouraged you.*

_____

_____

_____

You therefore, my son, be strong in the grace that is in Christ Jesus. The things that you have heard from me in the presence of many witnesses, entrust these to faithful men who will be able to teach others also.
2 Timothy 2:1-2 (ESV)

Jesus entrusts us with those He loves, He is entrusting us to spread the Good News that He came to save us, and He is entrusting us with His Word to be faithful and to learn to live by it daily.

Day 5: What Does Trust Mean for Me?

*Trust in the LORD with all your heart and
lean not on your own understanding; in all
your ways acknowledge him, and he will
make your paths straight.*
PROVERBS 3:5-6

**God has been and
will always be
worthy of
our trust**

Trust is an intimate expression and emotion to offer someone. We evaluate carefully those whom we deem worthy of our trust. God has been and will always be worthy of our trust. Men and women will fail us—we will fail ourselves—but trusting in the Lord will carry us through it all. If we recognize and call out our pain, we can then hand it over to Jesus. If we hide or ignore our hurt and our pain, we become enslaved to it.

1. Who do you trust in your life?

_____
_____
_____

2. Who do you find difficult to trust?

_____
_____
_____

3. What are some areas or issues that have broken your trust in the past?

_____
_____
_____

4. In what areas of life are you withholding trust from God?

_____
_____
_____

5. *What circumstances in your life might God be using to get your attention back to Him?*

_____

_____

_____

6. *In what ways will your choice to trust deepen your walk with Jesus?*

_____

_____

_____

Trust is the foundation for choosing to love, obey, forgive, surrender, and sacrifice. If we choose to trust God, then making good choices becomes more natural, even when life doesn't make sense. It doesn't make sense for a man to walk on water like Peter did, but it does make sense that when he fell, he looked to the One who came to save. It doesn't make sense to give glory to God when we have to say goodbye to our loved ones, but it does make sense to trust God to use our pain for good on His timetable. Trust is being able to say, "It's okay if I don't understand. I know God does, and I know He will work it out for good!"

Trust is the foundation for choosing to love, obey, forgive, surrender, and sacrifice

Lord, may we look to You for every choice we are faced with. May we become a victor in our circumstances by choosing You. May every choice we make deepen our relationship with You. Thank you for being the example of love, obedience, forgiveness, surrender, sacrifice and trust that will never fail us. Thank you for loving us. May every choice we make reflect the pure essence of who you are.
Amen.

Credits

1. Corrie Ten Boom In The Book, Reflections Of God's ... text .., http://www.sermoncentral.com/illustrations/sermon-illustration-stories-forgiveness-63066.asp (accessed June 19, 2014).

2. A Christian God Can Work Through sermon, A Christian God Can ...http://www.sermoncentral.com/sermons/a-christian-god-can-work-through-nathan-johnson-sermon-on-christian-disciplines-127837.asp (accessed June 19, 2014).

3. Mary, Mother of Jesus: A Willing Servant...A Higher Calling, http://inspiredmagazine.org/2014/05/09/mary-mother-of-jesusa-willing-servant-a-willing-servant/ (accessed June 19, 2014).

4. Goodrick, Edward W., and John R. Kohlberger III, and James A Swanson. *The Strongest NIV Exhaustive Concordance.* Grand Rapids: Zondervan, 2001.
   *** for further information see 3985-3986 (p. 1635)

5. Mark #9: Surrender and Self-Sacrifice | Bible.org, https://bible.org/seriespage/mark-9-surrender-and-self-sacrifice (accessed June 19, 2014).

6. *Goodrick, Edward W., and John R. Kohlberger III, and James A. Swanson. The Strongest NIV Exhaustive Concordance. Grand Rapids: Zondervan, 2001.*
   ****for further information see 3860 (p. 1633)*

7. Sacrifice - Definition and More from the Free Merriam-Webster .., http://www.merriam-webster.com/dictionary/sacrifice (accessed June 19, 2014).